Moving to Goa

KATHARINA KAKAR

PENGUIN BOOKS

An imprint of Penguin Random House

PENGUIN BOOKS

USA | Canada | UK | Ireland | Australia
New Zealand | India | South Africa | China

Penguin Books is part of the Penguin Random House group of companies
whose addresses can be found at global.penguinrandomhouse.com

Published by Penguin Random House India Pvt. Ltd
4th Floor, Capital Tower 1, MG Road,
Gurugram 122 002, Haryana, India

Penguin
Random House
India

First published in Viking by Penguin Books India 2013
This edition published in Penguin Books by Penguin Random House India 2023

ISBN 9780143461685

Typeset in Garamond by R. Ajith Kumar, New Delhi
Printed at Replika Press Pvt. Ltd, India

www.penguin.co.in

MIX
Paper from
responsible sources
FSC® C016779

Contents

Introduction   vii

1. Moving to Goa   1
2. Corner of Paradise   15
3. Sex on the Beach   29
4. My Village   41
5. Where the Arrow Struck   55
6. Houses of Chandor, Houses of Loutolim   65
7. Village Rituals   77
8. The Stoned Pig—Hippies and Neo-hippies   87
9. Nustiyachi Koddi: Fish Curry and Rice   105
10. Moving towards Christmas   119
11. Sacred Groves in Secret Forests   129
12. The Curse of the Red Gold Rush   145
13. Visiting the Migrant Gods   161
14. Horses, Slaves and Women   179
15. Monsoon Raga   195
16. How Foreign Is Foreign?   207

Acknowledgements   227

GOA

KEY

- Portuguese-occupied area in 1510—the Ilhas
- Area added to old conquests in 1543
- Extent of talukas

Map not to scale

Introduction

I have always had a passion for stories, legends and travelogues that shed light on a specific culture, its people and their ways of living and thinking. I am more interested in the *petites histoires*, as the French call them, stories that revolve around anecdotes, experiences and observations, in contrast to the *grand récit*, which tackles a theme in its historical complexity, order and totality. In my experience, it is the *petites histoires* that allow us to see the colours and shades of a culture, giving a sharper insight into the layers, patterns and unique characteristics of a place. As my husband Sudhir Kakar once wrote, 'The concreteness of the story, with its metaphoric richness, is perhaps a better path into the depths of emotion and imagination, into the core of man's spirit . . . the "melodic and scenic nature of inner life, the Proustian nature of memory and mind".'[1]

Looking into *petites histoires* does not mean losing sight of the 'bigger picture'. Otherwise the story to be told is in danger of remaining 'a mystifying jumble of trees without the pattern of the forest'.[2]

---

1 Sudhir Kakar, 'Intimate Relations'. *Exploring Indian Sexuality* (New Delhi: Penguin, 1989), p. 2.
2 Sudhir and Katharina Kakar, 'The Indians'. *India: Portrait of a People* (New Delhi: Penguin, 2007), p. 6.

Introduction

My account of Goa, where I have settled down and lived for the past ten years, is very personal. It is nurtured by my limitless curiosity to explore; and my love for the 'other', which has led me to travel around the world. It is reflected, too, in my deciding to study Asian religions and anthropology at university. Mine is the gaze of the outsider—the *bhaile*, as Goans call us—which at times also becomes that of an insider. It is a gaze of heartfelt love, but one that does not shy away from looking into the darker sides of Goan history and life. This book is my tribute to the people of this beautiful land, with its gleaming white churches, enchanting houses and its close-knit village communities; it is my quest to understand how they live, and the forces that shape their identity.

1

Moving to Goa

The train entered Margao railway station with an ear-splitting screech of brakes. After a twenty-seven-hour journey from New Delhi, we had finally arrived. Exhilaration trumped tiredness as Sudhir and I, our housekeeper, Kailash, his wife and two sons, and our dog piled into two taxis for our new home in the village of Benaulim, a few kilometres away. The house had been under renovation for many months and we did not expect to move into a finished home with every screw in place. But to find it at the same stage as I had last seen it four months earlier came as a shock. The floors were yet to be laid and the electric wiring was still to be done. Toilet fittings, still in their original packing, were stacked in what was to be the living room but was at this moment a totally unlivable room. There we stood, with boxes of personal belongings, pieces of luggage and a confused dog in a dusty, messy house unfit for human habitation, surrounded by a handful of construction workers who were looking at us as if we had arrived from Mars. We had no clue what to do next.

Exhausted after weeks of work, travelling and packing up two households—our flat in Berlin and the one in Delhi—I looked wordlessly at Sudhir before finally blurting out, 'Let's just get out of here for a few days.' I needed to recharge my batteries in order to deal with this situation. So that's what we did. Kailash offered to stay back with our belongings, while we moved for three days into a nearby beach hotel to swim, eat highly spiced seafood and go for long walks on the beach—the stuff of a Goa dream vacation for middle-class India. After this relaxing break, we returned to the house, rolled up our sleeves and, with the help of Eric, our construction supervisor, hired thirty construction workers, who camped, cooked and converted our garden into a public toilet for the next three months.

In 2002, when the idea of moving back to India took shape, we were both living in Cambridge, Massachusetts. We had no desire to move back to one of the polluted Indian metropolises with their traffic snarls, aggressive drivers and an infrastructure constantly teetering on the brink of collapse. Sudhir wanted good Internet connectivity and, because he travels a great deal, a place that was well connected by air. I was dreaming of the ocean and a wild garden. Goa seemed our best bet. Besides its bonus of natural beauty, it met both our minimum demands as a place in which to finally settle down. We decided to spend our ten-day spring break from Harvard on the sandy beaches of north Goa to figure out if we would actually like living here. We had no idea what to expect. I had not been to Goa for more than ten years, and Sudhir for more than twenty. Since our Easter vacation was short, I had contacted a real-estate broker through the Internet. In 2002, it was still possible to find an old Portuguese-style house in Goa that we could afford. As is the wont of real-estate brokers, for the first four days, our man mostly showed us houses which were ruins he had not been able to get rid of for many years, even to innocents like us. In the last three days of our stay, the places he showed us became more interesting. We had come with the intention of getting a 'feel' of Goa, to drive around its villages and explore the area beyond its famed beaches, but we certainly did not expect to leave with a signed contract to buy a house. The very last house we saw is the one we are living in today.

For several years, we had spent our winters in Delhi and summers in Berlin. As Sudhir wrote in his recently published memoir, 'We were both tired of the nomadic life with its European summers that had appeared so attractive at first glance. One never knew which books or clothes were where. More important, the regular move from one country to another distanced us from friends in both Berlin and Delhi. Since we were away for months, we could not become completely absorbed in their concerns and day-to-day lives that had continued in our absence. The gaze of the anthropologist was forcing itself into our eyes that only wished to be those of close friends.'[1] We were now ready to plunge into a different life, grow new roots, redefine our priorities, and exchange the buzz of city life for the tranquillity of village life, lulled by the soothing sound of swaying coconut palms.

The suddenness of our decision took my friends by surprise. Their responses ranged from enthusiasm to doubts about my sanity. Friends who had known me as a night owl and city girl, expressed amazement that I was voluntarily giving up my academic career and the stimulation of city life with its restaurants, concerts and other lively cultural offerings for a village where only the disappearance of a pig or the petty fights of the neighbours would make up our day's headlines. To cut a long story short, yes, of course I do miss the buzz at times. But surrounding yourself with books and living a creative life, attracting people you want to spend time with, can be done anywhere in this global world—

1 Sudhir Kakar, *A Book of Memory: Confessions and Reflections* (New Delhi: Penguin, 2011), p. 303.

especially in a place like Goa, where we are never short of friends and interesting visitors dropping in. And, anyway, I get out often enough to India's metropolises or abroad to refuel the part of me that is hungry for well-conceptualized art exhibitions and stimulating discussions. So neither my husband nor I have ever regretted the step we have taken, to live in a village among people whose lives are so different from ours and whose concerns we do not necessarily share. If we had found, over time, that Goa was not the place we imagined, we would simply have turned around and moved in a different direction. We share an attitude, which Sudhir once defined very succinctly when he said, 'I'd rather regret what I have done, than regret what I have *not* done.' Luckily we have nothing to regret. We simply love being here.

~

In May 2003, at the peak of the heat when one needs a couple of cold showers to survive the day, we settled into the half-renovated rooms of our 100-year-old farmhouse. It took a long and trying three months, in the middle of our first Goan monsoon, for our house to be finally ready. And this did not happen without daily battles, when I tried to make our workers reverse their usual daily routine of extended breaks with short periods of work in between. I could easily have been lecturing them on how to land on the moon or how to bake a thin-crust pizza for all the difference it made to their work routines. They had already made up their mind that I was an odd kind of white memsahib and should thus be ignored.

I got this reputation within the first week, when I decided that the garbage and construction debris strewn around the acre of ground surrounding the house needed to be cleared away. None of the workers was willing to do this. They pretended they had no idea of what I was trying to say. My Hindi is fairly poor, but this was not a language problem. It was their way of getting the message across to me that they were labourers, not ragpickers. They were polite, they listened and they nodded, saying 'Yes madam, no madam,' only to continue doing things their own way. Between the choice of getting upset or simply doing the job myself, I felt the latter option was more practical. So I went into the nearby town of Margao, bought a pair of rubber boots to protect myself against snakes and scorpions, grabbed a few empty cement bags that were lying around, and in the following three days, filled almost twenty of them, clearing every square metre of our land.

One morning, when Sudhir and I were about to leave the house to drive up to north Goa to meet our architect, I observed two of our construction workers with a rope, trying to pull down a dead palm tree which had lost its crown and was in danger of falling once the monsoon winds started to blow. Their uncoordinated efforts looked quite unprofessional; nor did my confidence grow when I saw a *feni* bottle being handed from one to the other. A strong local liquor brewed from the cashew fruit when it is ripening (or else from coconut), feni is fairly inexpensive and is consumed in almost the same quantity as water. When I politely voiced my concern that the tree trunk might fall on the newly constructed pillar of our garage, the professional pride of the workers was hurt. 'Madam, we can handle this, no worries,' they reassured me in a mix of Hindi and English. Half a dozen workers then gathered around the tree and a passionate discussion ensued on how to get the dead palm tree down without causing any damage, while another feni bottle appeared and made the rounds. On that note we left. When we returned home around half past four in the afternoon, it was to find that the tree had indeed fallen on the pillar, which had collapsed under its weight. No one had removed the tree or started to rebuild the pillar in our absence. Instead, the workers were sitting near it, happily drinking tea and playing cards. 'But madam,' one of them said calmly, when I finally lost my cool, 'if we had removed the trunk, you would not have *seen*.' I should surely understand that they had no choice but to remain sitting, enjoying their tea, since neither Eric, their supervisor, nor Sudhir and I were at the construction site to witness the regrettable accident. If they had cleaned up and reconstructed the pillar in our absence, we might have come to the conclusion that they had done nothing the whole day. On that unspoken note, now that I had *seen*, they worked furiously for all of thirty minutes, till at five o'clock sharp, all work came to its daily standstill.

My husband, meanwhile, had unpacked his laptop in a quiet corner of the veranda, signalling that this was not a world with which he was prepared to engage.

Pressed by the monsoon that was scheduled to arrive in a month's time, I complained so vehemently and so frequently to Eric that he started to run away as soon as he saw me. I liked Eric. He was a nice, helpful man who tried his best. It was only much later, having seen how things work in Goa, that I could fully appreciate how well he had done his job. At the time, I was still in the grip of my German expectations of efficiency and my behaviour must have tried him sorely. However, my persistent 'cracking of the whip' at the construction site finally led to some changes: instead of ten men working while the other twenty took a break or pretended to be busy by merely standing around a 'happening' place, now twenty men worked, while the remaining ten were busy doing nothing.

Several years later, I came across the book *Glad Seasons in Goa*, where Frank Simoes has a hilarious description of how his neighbour Colonel Jeremiah Saldanha tried to build a wall to protect his chickens from a mongoose. Observing labourers unloading a truck full of laterite stones, Simoes writes, 'They work for an hour and a half with toilet breaks, cigarette breaks, water breaks and mysterious, inexplicable disappearances. At the end of it all, one-third of the truck is unloaded. Colonel Saldanha calls the proceedings to a halt. Time, he says benignly, for lunch.'[2] Listening over the years to tales of similar tribulations from friends, I realized that this was not just my personal initiation into settling down in Goa but everyone's, no matter whether you are an 'Indian outsider' or a *firangi*. Time and work ethic have different meanings in the land of the Blue Mountains.

~

When we signed the contract to buy our house, it was freshly whitewashed and looked almost ready for us to move in. We loved its clay-tiled roof, the old wooden doors with iron latches, the carved windows and—when stepping inside—the open view into the roof without a false ceiling, which made the living room look almost like a small chapel. The house was huge, with more rooms than we needed and a beautiful veranda opening into the garden. The old crocket mud walls, almost a metre thick, were radiating

---

2 Frank Simoes, *Glad Seasons in Goa* (New Delhi: Penguin, 1994), pp. 143–4.

warmth and imperfection with their uneven finish. We simply fell in love with it. But beneath that charming outward veneer, the house was about to crumble. We discovered only later that a great part of it had to be dismantled and rebuilt. Eventually, the only parts of the original house that remained standing were the wonderful old walls. If it is true that most houses in Goa in the pre-1960s were made from mud, and only the *bhatkar* (landlord) houses were made of stone, then ours was a humble bhatkar house. The walls are built with layers of red laterite stones on the outside and stuffed with mud in between, a natural insulation against the heat of the summer, allowing the walls to breathe. Such walls not only have stories to tell, but have a totally different 'feel' to them compared to newly constructed houses. The coconut tree rafters of our roof, called *maddanche vanxe* by the villagers, as well as all the teak doors, had been hollowed out by white ants; most of the Mangalore roof tiles needed replacement; the wiring had to be redone, since the village electrician had never heard of the need for 'earthing'; the traditional red cement floor with a tile form pressed on it was too broken to be retained; the veranda needed extension; the windows were to be redone with traditional oyster frames and so on and so forth. I was especially keen on restoring the original 'nacre' windows, made of thin layers of oyster shell, trimmed into squares and fitted between vertical wooden slats.[3] This was a beautiful indigenous substitute for glass, the latter, in earlier times, only being accessible to very rich families since it had to be imported. With these windows, one does not need curtains, since they let in a soft filtered light when closed. If one

3 See Maurice Hall, *Window on Goa* (London: Quiller Press, 1992), p. 32–3.

likes the sun and air to enter the rooms, the window slats can be opened fully. A few years after we finished renovating our house, the use of nacre was prohibited due to the dwindling of oysters, one of the many environmental problems Goa is facing in the twenty-first century. We also rebuilt the *balcão*, a roofed veranda with built-in benches or seats, which comprises the front entrance of a Goan house, from where steps lead to a pillared porch. The balcão seats are where people sit and chat with their neighbours or family members, making it the most essential outdoor living area in Catholic houses.

It is interesting to note that the upper classes, the former Goan elite, did not reside in cities, but were village based. Thus, the more humble village houses like ours took their inspiration from the great mansions often described as Indo-Portuguese architecture. I actually disagree with the popular term 'Indo-Portuguese', since these houses are a unique development of Goan architecture over time, despite several features being inspired by Mediterranean architecture from Portugal, Italy and France. We were lucky enough to have found Dean de Cruz, a wonderful architect with a sensitive eye and exceptionally good taste. Only later, after hearing several horror tales from people renovating their new homes as innocently and ignorantly as we did, did we realize how lucky we were that Dean and his team had worked so reliably and honestly, and done work of such quality.

~

With every passing week the monsoon came closer, and our house was gradually becoming more habitable. We now had running water and a shower, the kitchen was functional and a stove was bought. Kailash was finally able to cook his delicious meals without tearing his hair out, and we did not have to go out for dinner that often. Meanwhile, I learned how to lay a mosaic floor in typical Goan style, making use of broken and leftover floor tiles. The tradition of Goan mosaic floors has survived from the time when trading vessels returning home with a full cargo of spices dumped broken Chinese porcelain, which had served as ballast, on Goa's shores. In some of the old houses one can still see pieces of beautiful Chinese crockery worked into the flooring as mosaic. To the horror of our workers, I bought brand-new tiles, which they had to smash to pieces. As if that was not enough, I insisted I would work with them since I had my own definite ideas on the pattern of the mosaic in the entrance hall. With a mix of unease and amusement they taught me how to lay a mosaic—a skill which came in handy later, when I used it to build a small temple and a tea house close to the veranda where Sudhir sits and works every morning.

Between May and August 2003, when the renovation of our house was in full swing, two thefts took place. First, my gold ring disappeared. I blamed myself for having left it near the bathroom window, unaware that anyone passing by could just reach in and grab it. We did nothing, because we did not want to get twenty-nine out of thirty innocent workers into trouble with the police who, as in the rest of the country, are in the habit of first beating up and then asking questions. I consoled myself, thinking that whoever had stolen the ring needed it more than I did. But when a few weeks later our bronze statue disappeared overnight, we knew we had to do something about it. Sudhir had gifted me that beautiful sculpture shortly before we moved to Goa. It was a creation of the well-known artist Radhakrishnan—a happy and expressive sculpture of a woman, bent down like an animal and stretching one hand towards the sky. She was so heavy that two strong men would have had difficulty lifting her. But obviously the thieves were resourceful. Instead of calling the local police station—which most probably would have made it difficult to ever get her back—we pulled some strings with the help of friends. As a result, the policemen were given orders by someone high up the ladder in the police hierarchy. Within hours, a dozen constables showed up at our house, interviewing neighbours and swinging into action. The presence of so many men in uniform did not go unremarked. As we had hoped, the message that it is better not to mess with these outsiders who have just moved here, had done its rounds. It was fairly clear to us that the statue was not stolen by art lovers, but because of its metal value. Policemen showed a photograph of the sculpture to all scrap dealers in the vicinity, warning them of dire consequences if they happened to find our lady on their premises. Whoever had hidden her under a haystack or in a cowshed, now had no way of disposing of her. Only two days later, the milkman—one of the prime suspects— just 'happened' to find her lying in a ditch a kilometre away from our house. He informed our neighbour, who informed us, and we happily reclaimed our sculpture and brought it home. We have not had a problem with theft since then.

We experienced our first Goan monsoon in our new house, its restoration finally complete, and exulted in the way it regreened the land. And now we looked forward to our first winter season, when guests would arrive and we would finally have the time and the right weather to explore our new homeland. Looking back ten years later, despite my periodic frustration about inefficiency and unreliability when it comes to work and commitments, I have to admit that Goa has exceeded my expectations. What makes me feel so comfortable here? From a personal point of view, it is the peace we have found here. The mornings start with yoga, or a walk on the beach, followed by a steaming cup of coffee, before we retire to our desks to write or to do other chores in and around the house. The house is no longer just our private living habitat, but also serves as an office for my NGO, Tara Trust, with volunteers walking in and out, working on projects in community schools and for the welfare of children in the nearby slums.

Goa is our chosen home now. I believe that the most important decisions in one's personal life are taken somewhere in the diffused and hidden landscape of one's inner self. For Sudhir and me, moving to Goa has been such a decision—it happened before we even knew it.

2

Corner of Paradise

In the years that have followed, people often wonder how we managed to find such a perfect house in such an idyllic location just by driving around with a real-estate broker for less than a week. Today, with hundreds of Goans claiming to be 'brokers' (one of the many businesses in Goa in which a fast buck can be made), Goa is on the verge of being 'sold out'. Indeed, today it is almost impossible to find an attractive and affordable house, not to speak of one with a big garden. Ironically, the same Goans who benefit hugely by acting as brokers to foreigners and Indians from outside Goa are the ones bemoaning the 'selling out' of Goa. They happily take the outsiders' money, but resent the *bhaile*—the outsider—buying Goan property, blaming them for spoiling land prices and taking over Goan soil.

Ten years back, it was still possible to find a beautiful house, though I am always tempted to say that we did not find our house—it found us. When we decided to settle in Goa, we did not even know the difference between south and north Goa. We came for a week, bought a house with an acre of palm trees almost on an impulse, and realized only later that its location not only suited us much better than a house in the 'happening' north Goa with its restaurants, parties and hectic social life, but also that all the house papers were in order. This is a nightmare in the majority of land transactions in Goa where such sales are governed by both Indian and Portuguese law. The former owner, an elderly Portuguese–Goan—an Indian gentleman with a Portuguese passport and Portuguese ancestors—had bought the house from a woman who had moved away when she decided to live with her daughter in Bangalore. This lady had lived in it for ages, running a kindergarten, as I was told years later by a visitor who recognized the place from his childhood days. All houses in Goan villages have names by which they are locally known, and anyone in the neighbourhood will be able to point out a house if one asks for it by its intimate name. Our house was called 'snail house' (*kongo*), as our neighbours informed me, and thus the earlier owner was the 'snail-lady'. We never met our snail-lady, though she once came back to Goa when we were away travelling. My neighbour Tina told me later that she was touched and happy to see her house still standing and well cared for, instead of being torn down, as is the fate of so many of these old beauties, to make place for flats or ugly modern bungalows. We still have a reclining chair that belonged to her, with her initials '*A.F.*' on it, the only piece of furniture that was left in the house when we moved in. It is a chair that we use every day, when we are sitting out in the veranda in the evenings.

Mr Afonso, who sold us the house, intended to retire here, but later thought that maintaining such an old house would be too much for him, especially since his two daughters who were living abroad had no intention of moving back to Goa. So, for many years until we arrived, it remained empty and uncared for.

Many years of abandonment had turned the garden into a sandy wasteland, since there is no rain in Goa for eight months after the monsoon is over. Only the hardy coconut palms and fruit trees with deep roots, such as mango, jackfruit, guava and chikoo, a few wild bushes and one huge cactus had survived. The latter produced the most gorgeous white flowers once the monsoon started. I was delighted by all the different fruit trees, including a slim local one with thorns that produces black sour berries. I was unable to find out its name, since my garden books did not have its picture, and my neighbours shrugged their shoulders in ignorance. I called it the blue-berry tree and enjoy watching the birds eating its fruits. Of the chikoos that grow in abundance like small round potatoes on the tree outside our bedroom window, we have not been able to eat even one in the last ten years—squirrels, birds and bats feast on them before they are fully ripe. Guava trees, called *peram* by the locals, can be found in almost every compound. I love the smell of the ripe guava. Cut open, sprinkled with salt and chilli, it makes a delicious snack.

Once the renovation of the house ended, my interest in gardening awoke. It was a welcome diversion that took up a lot of my time in the first few years, since 5000 square metres of sandy land needed to be transformed into a garden. My idea of a garden is quite different from carefully tended lawns with neat flowerbeds. I prefer it semi-wild, more like a jungle garden, where I can experiment with different plants and fruits. I ordered truckloads of mud to mix with the sand, and bought so many plants at a nursery in Margao that the owner, a friendly elderly man, asked me one day, 'You still have space in your garden to walk?' Step by step, over the next few years, a jungle emerged, though I have to admit, nature did most of the makeover: one monsoon is enough to transform a piece of barren land into a tropical forest. Tiny plants grow overnight into big bushes, but as Sudhir observes, 'Even a jungle needs a lot of labour to look really wild.'

Kailash, as enthusiastic about gardening as I am, would have liked the garden to be much more orderly. He is especially bothered by the jamun tree, a beautiful tall tree, which must have been planted at least half a century ago. It has forked into multiple trunks, its leaves whispering in the breeze, its branches swaying in the wind. While Kailash complains about the chore of sweeping up its falling leaves, I am wondering how to make jamun-vinegar out of its fruit. The fruits, the colour of red wine and no bigger than oval cherries, cannot be plucked because the tree has now grown to such an enormous height. They can, however, be collected after they are ripe and have fallen to the ground.

For a long time, I also wondered what to do with the small coconuts the trader leaves behind after harvesting our coconut trees. I now sometimes crack them open, dry the white coco-meat, the *copra*, in the sun for a week or two, and then drive to a mill in a village nearby, with an old cement-sack full of dried coconuts and a few empty plastic bottles on the backseat of my car. It is quite an experience, though time-consuming, to sit with villagers on old wooden benches in a shed, where two electric mills grind coconuts for oil, another mill grinds rice and somewhere in the back, the scent of masala rises from a hammering spice mill. It is so loud that conversations soon come to a stop. I usually take a friend along to chat or have a cup of tea in the *chai*-shop next door, till it is our turn to press the oil. Posters of Jesus and Mary, of Hindu gods and of landscapes decorate one of the dusty walls. The villagers stare at me with friendly curiosity—I must be the only foreigner who has ever come to this traditional mill. At home, I mix the cold-pressed coconut oil with essential oils such as cinnamon or lemongrass and fill it in small bottles to gift to all my friends as massage oil. I would never have imagined during my years as an academic how much satisfaction I could get from such 'trivial' pursuits.

To work the soil with your own hands, to check on flowers and fruits towards which one had been fairly indifferent earlier, to maintain a constantly changing garden, or make massage oil out of dried coconut meat from one's own backyard, gives a pleasure difficult to describe. It is easy to fall into the trap of using clichés that praise nature's beauty and talk of one's closeness to 'Mother Earth'. Nevertheless, such clichés are as true as they are false because garden work is primarily hard labour, at times extremely frustrating and tiring, at others calming and rewarding. But what it surely does to me is a kind of 'weeding of my brain'. I return to my writing desk with new thoughts, or at least with the awareness of an open space within my head.

Digging the earth and watching over my flowers and bushes as they flourish is a pleasure I only discovered after moving to Goa, though I grew up with a garden in Germany. Finding out which plants were growing well over time, observing snakes, birds and insects, grounded me in nature—a feeling that will only be fully understood by those who are garden freaks themselves and cherish nature in all her infinite variety. Working in my garden has taught me to appreciate the smaller forms of life, such as butterflies, spiders, frogs, lizards and beetles. And indeed, there is so much to see if one only observes closely. I was amazed to discover how many different types of ants live in my garden and house—known locally as *umlo, domlo, valloi, katt-mui* and *chabkuri mui*. Some of them are tiny, others—big black ones—only come out at night, running around in our bathroom, disappearing mysteriously before dawn and at times leaving hundreds of white eggs in a hidden corner between towels or clothes. A mini-sized breed of black ants took a liking to our electrical wires, knocking out several wall sockets, till I placed mothballs behind all electrical switches to keep them at bay (yes, one has to deal with all such unexpected happenings in an old house built of mud and laterite stones). The ones I like least are the red weaver-ants, whose bites are agonizingly painful and who build their nests by gluing two or three leaves on a bush or tree together. At times, when my two cats leave some of their fish and rice in the feeding bowl on the veranda, an impressive army of red ants appears out of nowhere, carrying away morsels of fish and whole grains of rice.

Apart from snakes, birds and other mysterious creatures such as the olive-brown calotes (they look like miniature dragons and are one of the thirty species of lizards one finds in Goan gardens and jungles), there are some strange nocturnal animals. One of them is a wild black feline called a civet cat that actually looks like a big house cat with a long snout and a bushy tail. The locals call it *arando* or *azandor* and do not particularly like it. Our arando regularly visits the roof to chase squirrels. I believed for many years they raid the squirrels' nests for a tasty dinner, till a friend told me that they are pure vegetarians. Our arando sometimes leaves a pile of shit with seeds in it as a farewell gift, maybe as a reminder that it will be back another night. Now, if we had coffee bushes in our garden I might have made a fortune—coffee beans recovered from the excreta of civet cats are much prized and sell for an absolute fortune in Indonesia.

Sudhir and I spend more time on the veranda than inside the house, since we have placed our writing desks there and also our reclining chairs, where we read and relax. My desk faces the garden greenery, while Sudhir's overlooks an octagonal fountain, which I built for him a few years back. After a holiday in Andalusia in

Spain, with its Moorish-influenced architectural styles, we were both enchanted by the constant sound of running water from the many beautiful fountains in Cordoba and Seville. Later, walking in the streets of Delhi, I stumbled upon an adventurous potter who had encroached upon the pavement with a miniature tile-making factory. Without hesitation I placed my order, paid an advance, not really sure if the many hand-baked tiles would ever reach Goa. They did, each one carefully folded in newspaper and not a single one broken. This is how our fountain came into being. However, in true Goan style, it leaked from day one; the person who built it—an 'expert' in his field—was never seen again. It took us several years to find the root cause and fix it, but it was worth the trouble. Today we have kingfishers and a paradise flycatcher that take their daily baths in the fountain.

The number of birds that have made our garden their habitat once it grew into a jungle, giving them shelter, breeding space and food, astonished me. Regular guests in our garden are red-whiskered bulbuls, jungle babblers, blue flycatchers, paradise flycatchers, coucals, koels, kingfishers, cuckoos, golden orioles, starlings, tree pies, large green barbets (so camouflaged, one thinks they are part of the tree), magpie-robins and drongos. There are also woodpeckers, tailorbirds, purple-rumped sunbirds with their yellow bellies and many others. None of them was here when we first moved into our house with its sandy wasteland of a garden. We even have a pair of crimson sunbirds. They are tiny with a ruby-red belly and usually live in jungles. They feed, like the purple-rumped sunbirds, on the nectar of flowers. Last year I saw them raising a baby bird. I watched the parents using different strategies to teach and encourage their grown baby to feed from the flowers. For more than three weeks the baby terrorized its parents (and me) with its shrieking calls for

food, instead of giving it a try himself. The bushes and flowers
my crimson sunbirds feed on grow right in front of my writing
desk, so I could observe them at close quarters. A bird one meets
everywhere in Goa, especially on the beach, but rarely in our garden,
is the black crow—they are not my favourite, since I can't stand the
sound of their call. I have trained my dogs to chase them away. An
old Goan folk saying, however, holds that a crow cawing near the
house indicates that a relative, good news or a letter will arrive soon.

Of great beauty also are the many butterflies that have found
their way into our garden. I recently started to take an interest
in planting flowers and shrubs that are especially attractive to
butterflies, and learned from a nearby butterfly farm in Ponda,
run by an engaging Goan couple, that butterflies love to suck on
local papaya (called 'tree melons' by Europeans when they first
encountered papayas several hundred years ago). Butterflies also
like beer and overripe bananas. I do not know the names of our
butterflies—but I have seen at least twenty or thirty different
species in our garden, some of them very beautiful. The only
species I can identify are the Plain Tiger, the Malabar Raven and
the Blue Mormon, a huge astonishing black-and-blue butterfly,
which is a regular in our garden and a true eye-catcher. We do not
use pesticide and have a profusion of local flowers and plants for
them to feed on, so the environment our garden offers seems to
suit them well. For the past three years, we have even had fireflies
appearing in August—an indicator of ecological balance, though
they are just a handful and not the thousands I had seen when I
walked with Buddhist monks through villages in Bihar twenty-
five years ago.

Our garden also has snakes. Most of them are huge, almost
two-metre-long rat snakes, which love to feast on small frogs and

toads. They often come quite close to the house. This year one of my cats caught a bronze-back tree snake, a slim creature with bright blue spots and dark intense eyes. I chased the cat away by throwing a coconut at it, but did not dare touch the snake. Since it refused to move away, I called the forest department for help.

In Goa, there are many young people who are engaged in wildlife and environmental programmes and take enthusiastic part in animal-rescue missions. In 2010, the most exciting rescue in our area was that of a pangolin in Orlim, a neighbouring village. Pangolins—locally called *sheryo*—look like cute walking pine cones. They have the face of an ant-eater and burrow their sharp claws into ant and termite mounds to feed on these insects. Curled up, they look like an artichoke with a tail. Before I read about the pangolin rescue in the papers, I did not even know that such strange-looking mammals, covered with keratin scales, existed in Goa.

Within ten minutes of my snake-rescue call, Benhail, a young man who lives in my village, arrived on his motorcycle. He blithely picked up the slightly injured snake, which slithered round his hand while he typed notes into his mobile phone. Even I picked up enough courage to hold the snake, though not without that particular unease with which one holds a newborn baby for the first time.

Our spread-out garden houses a great variety of plants, many of which I have also seen in Sri Lanka, Singapore and Malaysia. Amitav Ghosh, one of my favourite Indian writers, who has recently decided to live part of the year in the Goan village of Aldona, writes in his novel *River of Smoke* about the journey of botanists and plants from and to China. One tends to forget that most of the vegetables, fruits and a wide range of plants that we associate with Goa or Asia today are not indigenous, many of them coming from South America, having travelled to India with the Portuguese from their colonies there 500 years ago. Even the chilli—so much a part of Goan and Indian cuisine now—was unknown to India before the arrival of the Portuguese. There are just a few plants that found their way to Goa in pre-colonial times, one of them being the *baobab*, a native of Africa. This 'upside-down-tree' with its thick grey trunk and giant-sized sour fruit, lives for hundreds of years and was cherished for its medicinal value by Arab merchants, who planted them in Goa. Today, one of the few baobab trees left grows near the governor's house in Dona Paula and a small grove can also be found at Sulabhat in Goa Velha,[1] which used to be an Arab settlement long before the Portuguese arrived on Goa's shores. Another baobab tree grows in the front garden of a friend's house in Morjim. It is gigantic and my friend believes that his ancestors brought it back as a seed from Africa. When I examined its leaves and fruits closely, I realized that the beautiful fruits were tied to the lower branches with a thin thread. 'Oh,' he said with a smile on his face, 'my father does this. He loves these fruits so much, he picks them up when they fall and ties them back to the tree.'

Other plants, I imagine, found their way into Goa through Goan migrants, who had lived and worked in Portuguese colonies in Africa and travelled back home with a few seeds and bulbs in their suitcases. One of these African wonders is the blood lily, native to South Africa, which is one of my favourite flowers. It blooms once a year with the beginning of the rains and transforms

---

1 See Pratima P. Kamat, *Goa, Its Tryst with Trade* (Panaji: Goa Chamber of Commerce and Industry, 2009), p. 21.

one of my flowerbeds into a sea of bright red blossoms the size of oranges. Having seen them in many front gardens of old Goan houses, I tried for years to buy them in local nurseries, but without success. One day, when visiting the well-known Goan artist and writer Savia Viegas in Carmona, one of our neighbouring villages, I saw a cluster of these beauties on an empty plot of land beside a crumbling house. I came back the next day equipped with hoe and spade and started digging out the bulbs. My activities attracted many villagers, who thought there must be buried treasure in the ground if a Western woman was sweating and working so hard to get to it. It wasn't long before they called a man from the panchayat. He came up to me with an expression of grave suspicion on his face but broke into laughter when I showed him what I had found.

Exploring Goa and getting to know my unfamiliar new home in the first years after we settled here, involved many experiments in my garden, trying to grow a variety of plants and fruits, including those available in local markets. I discovered the many varieties of bananas that grow here (called *rasabali, saldatti, lal velchi, moindolli*), the best being cooking-bananas grown around the village of Moira. I tasted many different mangoes, of which the most delicious varieties are the Alfonso and the Malcorada, drafted by Jesuit priests, who contributed greatly to Goan agriculture. I dug out many unknown and humble plants from the side of the road (for a while I always had a shovel in my car) and planted them in my garden. I bought spice plants, such as cinnamon, nutmeg and pepper, and take joy in the many fragrant bushes and trees, such as my yellow champa trees or the *raat ki rani* (queen of the night) with its numerous white flowers that open at night and wrap everything around in a heady perfume.

Among the many things my years in Goa have taught me is that the pleasure one takes in the small things of daily life, the engagement with one's surroundings, the awareness of being in the moment, is what defines the quality of one's life. My garden, always in transformation, is a constant reminder that life is a journey to explore and enjoy, not a destination to reach.

3

Sex on the Beach

A place that becomes less of a journey and more of a destination for most foreign tourists, however, is the beach and they rarely move beyond its sun-'n'-sand-'n'-surf pleasures. They escape the miserable winter months in Europe, Russia and other cold parts of the world, and see little of Goa beyond their chosen beach for their entire holiday. They come to relax and soak up the sun, to get away from the stressful pace of their lives at home and take in a little bit of Goan *susegad*. Nothing wrong with that. Most of them, however, do not take part in the drugs-and-sex scene for which Goa's beaches have gained a notorious reputation.

Most Goans are outraged by the state's reputation as a haven for junkies and sex-trippers. Whether it is the sensational case of fifteen-year-old Scarlett Keeling, a British teenager who was allegedly drugged, raped and murdered on Anjuna beach in February 2008, or other headlines relating to sun, sex and surf that make national and international news, Goans are very prickly about anything that highlights sexual permissiveness or questionable morals in Goa. In 2011, for example, the Hindi movie *Dum Maaro Dum* that depicted the Goan drug mafia made headlines in local newspapers even before it was released, because its trailer carried a line referring to Goan women as being 'cheap' ('Over here . . . liquor is cheap, and the women are cheaper . . .'). Eventually, the producers agreed to cut parts of the dialogue that offended so many Goans. Another recent example is the response to *Tehelka* editor Tarun Tejpal, who in November 2011, jokingly remarked during the opening of the Think Fest in Bambolim, 'Now you are in Goa, drink as much as you want, eat . . . sleep with whoever you think of . . .' The response from the local media and 'concerned citizens' ranged from disgust to boiling anger, and his remark was quoted so often that I stopped counting.

Why do Goans react so violently to such perceptions? The real Goa, as Goans perceive it, is a place of 'deep social conservatism, of folk religiosity in its village temples and churches, of simplicity of lifestyle . . . and of immense pride in its plural, multi-cultural heritage'.[1] I have lived long enough in Benaulim to have seen for myself the importance people in my village give to caring for the extended family and protecting their children, especially their daughters. In that respect they are no different from families in the rest of India. Most visitors are not aware of the day-to-day life of the common man in Goa, their customs and rituals, the things that engage and interest them or the beauty of the state's hinterland, because they rarely move beyond the beach belt. For them, the plurality of voices and diversity of lifestyles will remain a blank spot.

Nevertheless, sex, drugs and raves on the beach are also a slice of Goan reality, a facet of *Goa Dourada*, the Golden Goa, that cannot be denied. Along with foreign backpackers and young Indians visiting from other states, Goan youth too are a part of this Goa. And casual sex is not confined to tourists alone—it is also widespread among locals and visiting youngsters from other

---

1 Jason Keith Fernandes, 'Of Rapes, Murder, Drugs and the "Real Goa"', in *Gomantak Times*, 26 March 2008, p. A8.

Indian states. Take, for example, the many young waiters who work in the beach shacks during the season—local youngsters as well as migrants from Nepal, Darjeeling, Rajasthan and other places. For them, the attraction of the job is not the hard work and bad pay, but the many opportunities they get to hit on European girls. Ever since we moved to Benaulim, Sudhir and I have been frequenting three beach shacks for a sunset drink or dinner. Over the years, watching the beach boys grow and listening to their stories, we have become good friends with many of them. They told me that in one particular beach shack in north Goa, the waiters have put up a world map on the kitchen wall, and each time a waiter successfully seduces a girl (or claims to have done so), he pins a needle to the respective country of his conquest.

When I started writing this book, I asked some of the waiters we have known for years if they would agree to be interviewed and if they would speak frankly. All of them agreed: the condition was that they had to be shamelessly honest about their views and experiences. But I won't reveal the most interesting stories, as those would give away their identities. At one of the shacks where we are regulars, the boys have a system of competing among themselves for the girls. There is an unwritten rule that the waiter who first gets into a conversation with a girl showing the slightest interest in him, such as listening to what he has to say, will be the one who will serve her again if she comes back the next day. This way there is a hope of 'deepening' the relationship. Surprisingly, the charms and methods of the beach boys prove to be quite effective. Needless to say, their targets are only women without male companions, though the age of the woman is no bar. The range of conquests among lonely women looking for sex varies from (preferably) young and beautiful girls to sixty-plus, (preferably) generous and well-to-do women. Once the new waiters gain confidence, often with the help of an older woman in their first or second season, they try their luck with younger women. They soon find out that it is easiest to hit on young girls, because, explains one waiter, 'after twenty-five they are too experienced and ask too many questions'.

The transformation of a first-season beach boy into a confident Casanova is a long journey full of hurdles. 'You have to learn to read the signals,' said one good-looking veteran. He added—and this was confirmed by others—'Almost all of us have our first "experience" with an older woman.' He told me about foreign women twice or thrice the age of the young waiter, often staying for weeks or months at the beach, initiating him and his colleagues into the art of sex. One of these women is a divorced, educated, sixty-plus lady. I have met her, since she comes back every year and always stays at the same beach shack which has become a second home to her. I would never have guessed that she had a sizzling secret life! Indeed, sexual encounters between women aged forty to sixty with waiters who are still virgins is pretty common. But unlike other tourist hotspots such as Thailand or Tunisia where prostitution of young males is common, waiters in Goa do not prostitute themselves. For all my interviewees, having 'done it' with an older woman is simply an entry point into their own sexual life, a necessary initiation to gain enough confidence to interact with attractive young women.

However, before the newcomer ventures into his 'first experience' with a mother-lover, he usually suffers through a range of innocent passions, like the young man who fell madly in love with a thirteen-year-old Russian girl staying with her parents at the beach shack. He recounted to me that he hardly ate for days and could not think about anything else but his Russian beauty, though he never spoke to her and their communication did not go beyond eye contact. 'Does she know?' I asked him when he revealed his dilemma. 'I think so, she gave me that look,' he answered, looking down at his feet in embarrassment. A couple of weeks later, when his beauty had long returned home, he gathered enough courage to write to the parents, asking politely for a family photo. Her parents must have had a sense of humour: they promptly replied and sent him a picture of themselves and the girl's grandparents—the object of his adoration herself was missing from the photograph!

Goa's reputation as a land of free sex and endless parties began in the late 1960s 'when the first lot of hippies began to straggle into Anjuna and Arambol . . . They attracted only a cursory look from fishermen and toddy tappers. What were a few Whites zonked out on hallucinogens compared to the authoritarian Portuguese that ruled for 451 years?' writes journalist Devika Sequeira.[2] They were a bunch of self-absorbed, confused idealists, who were uninterested in local culture, customs or history. Although the villagers might have disapproved of their skimpy clothes and careless manners, they lodged them and took their money. It is the hippies who should get the credit for starting Goa's beach tourism, because sensational stories in Indian newspapers about naked youngsters from Europe and America dancing through the night acted like a magnet to hundreds of 'hippy-watchers', who travelled to Goa to have a closer look. Fifty years later, only a few hippies are left and a lot has changed. Sex on the beach and sex in the minds, however, has remained. Indian men, generally from a conservative background, still come in busloads during the

2   Devika Sequeira, 'Not a Sin City', in *Deccan Herald*, online (http://www.deccanherald.com/content/47169/not-sin-city.html).

tourist season to watch naked, pale flesh turning pink on beach-beds. They also see Goan girls in bars and clubs, talking to men who are neither their brothers nor their uncles, reinforcing their image of the 'cheap Goan woman', not to speak of their ideas of Western women, who they believe would like nothing more than to sleep with strangers like them. Any white woman moving around in Goa on her own will be lecherously targeted, as I have been countless times, once even when I was driving our car on the highway at noon, the windows down. A motorcycle zoomed up next to me and the driver shouted hysterically through the open window: 'Want to have sex? Want to have sex? Want to have sex?' I showed him the middle finger and he zoomed off. It was like a slapstick scene from a B-grade movie.

The beach boys, however, claim to be different from the sexually repressed, conservative Indian males who come to Goa's beaches in droves on weekends from the neighbouring states of Karnataka and Maharashtra, their eyes riveted on tourists in bikinis. Perhaps it would be more correct to say that the sexual attitudes of the beach boys change after the first couple of seasons, by when they have learned to read the cues and signals of foreign women, and have become adept at striking up relationships. As one of them, who prides himself on having around five affairs per season, told me, 'When I go out with friends and we meet some new girls and nothing much happens—no signals and signs—I leave.' He does not want to waste his time: 'It is less about feelings, it's really about sex,' he says. He admits that sometimes, if a girl stays on, he gets attached and develops tender feelings towards her. He does not like this, because the relationship then becomes complicated. In one such situation, the girl returned the next season and he had to handle her and his new affair at the same time. He slept with both, a situation which eventually put him in a lot of trouble with the two girls after they found out. He and the other beach boys emphasize that while they treat the girls with respect, these encounters are about having a good time with no strings attached. They claim that by and large, the girls and also the middle-aged or elderly women know the rules of the game with the beach boys—just a holiday fling, with no emotional involvement. 'But did you ever seriously fall in love with one of the girls?' I asked. Many of them said they had been through this experience, but learned their lesson when the girl went back to her own country and they were left heartbroken. When I asked them if they could imagine marrying a foreign girl, one of the young men came back with this memorable reply: 'Why buy the cow if you can milk it?'

Over the years, however, we have seen a few relationships between the beach boys and foreign women ending in marriage—usually with women around ten to fifteen years older and much better educated. The attraction here was simply the chance such a marriage gave to get out of the country, to make real money and secure their future and dreams abroad or back in India. Such women, say the beach boys I talked to, are regarded as a 'money tree' to be shaken. Often, though, it is beyond the young man's imagination to realize that moving to Europe will expose him to humiliating experiences and that his lack of education and exposure to harsh working conditions will also strain the relationship. And indeed, most marriages from such vastly different backgrounds do fail. As my conversations with the young men as well as the older women involved have revealed, when passion and sexual desire fade and the reality of day-to-day life sets in, the mismatched partners start to realize that they cannot overcome the barriers of their backgrounds and the culturally different expectations they have from each other. By the time this realization has dawned, the couple often has a child, making a break-up more difficult.

Clearly, one of the perks of a beach boy's job in Goa is an active and adventurous sex life. But where do they do it? I imagined it must be difficult to sneak in and out of rooms of the shack where they work without being noticed. 'Everywhere,' was the answer I got—'rooms, cars, showers, in the water.' They even do it at the back of the stalls where tourist items are sold during the day and which are just covered with a sheet of plastic at night, enough to give them some privacy. Then, there are the sand dunes slightly off the beach and at times, in the cover of night, on the beach itself. Often, if the girl is staying just for a few days or a week, the sex happens on the last day, before she is leaving for good. 'It takes time to talk and win her trust,' says one of them.

By and large they have affairs with westerners. Indian girls, though they may appear outwardly westernized, are mainly taboo—caste and class structures are still deeply ingrained in the Indian mind and these boundaries are hard to cross for both sides. The moment my questions were directed towards Indian girls, avoidance set in. The beach boys did not want to talk about them. Perhaps the thought of sex with an Indian girl brings their mothers and sisters back into their own conscience: what would they think if they only knew . . . thus leaving them uncomfortable about the boundaries they have crossed. The beach boys also find it much easier to be around and strike up a conversation with foreign girls and, as many of them pointed out, sex is not a big issue for them. Indian girls are for marriage, as one of them told me; Western girls are for fun.

The beach boys, even in their relationships with Western women, have their own code of conduct and pretty clear rules about dos and don'ts in public. Thus, while it's fine to display one's flab in the skimpiest bikini on the beach, they do not approve, for example, of Western tourists who go shopping or into restaurants in their swimwear, or who treat the beach restaurant like a dressing room. Often they are told to cover up or go into the bathroom to change. One of the waiters once went up to a woman sunbathing topless and told her to get dressed or leave (in south Goa, unlike north Goa and its old hippie hangouts, going topless on the beach is not common).

The beach boys I have known over the years in the different shacks Sudhir and I regularly go to are also very protective when they see foreign women being harassed or intrusively ogled by Indian men who travel to Goan beaches expressly for that purpose. 'Such men have a bikini problem,' observed one of the boys wearily. 'They only have TV experience with American girls and misunderstand,' he added.

One of the waiters, thin and very young when he came to Goa for the first time, told me how he dealt with his own physical arousal, never having seen half-naked white female bodies lying in the sun before. He was overwhelmed by this sight, but also shocked and confused by what this did to his own body. He did not know how to cope with his excitement. That first season, way too shy to approach one of the women on a beach-bed or in the restaurant, he often ran into the shack's toilet to jerk off, after which he continued serving his customers. Five years later, that same boy has a new avatar as he talks self-confidently about his erotic adventures and flaunts his body which he rigorously trains through bodybuilding exercises.

Many waiters have intriguing life stories, having moved to Goa from other parts of India to seek their fortune, and finally managing to turn their lives around. One of them, hailing from Rajasthan, was only fifteen when he fell in love with a girl from his village, who belonged to a different caste. The girl's clan threatened to kill him for his effrontery and he was forced to flee his village at night, hiding in a truck. For years he did not dare return home, doing odd jobs for a pittance in a number of places, including Bombay, until he fetched up in Goa. Now, after many years as a waiter, he has prospered. Together with a Goan partner, he runs his own beach shack in winter and a business in Ladakh in summer. Another one is a native of Goa, bright and good-looking, and an untiring Don Juan, if one believes the stories told about him. He took a risk to start his own business with the help of a foreigner a few years back. Today he spends a lot of his time in Bombay, taking classes in scriptwriting for films, and I would not be surprised if he finds success in this venture too. Most beach boys have a common story to tell—of poverty, joblessness at home and then finding their way to Goa, usually through someone in their village who takes them along and helps them get a job in a shack and a place to stay. For the beach boys, being in Goa is an adventure that also allows them to send some money home to the family. Add to that, as one beach boy told me, 'Free sex, good food and good times—why should we not like it here?'

Those too inhibited or timid to indulge in sex on the beach could just order the drink of the same name—it is sweet, heady and exists in many different variations. Here's the classic recipe: 1.5 oz vodka, 0.5 oz peach schnapps, 2 oz cranberry juice and 2 oz orange juice. Shake well and serve in a highball glass. Bon appétit!

4

My Village

Village life in Goa is almost completely unknown to the visitors who throng Goa's beaches. Goans claim that every village is known for something special: Sangolda for its variety of beans, Parra for its watermelons, Aldona for its chillies, Nerul for its groundnuts and sweet potatoes, Assagao for its flowers, Candolim for its salted fish, Cotula for its curry and Saligao for its sugarcane sweets.[1] My village, Benaulim—or Bannavli, as pronounced in Konkani—is known for its eccentrics, or, as the Goans frame it, its mad people. There is only one other village up north with the same reputation: Moira. 'No wonder you moved here,' said a dear friend, smiling mischievously. And indeed, Benaulim has a number of weird people wandering its streets. One of them is Calculator, who owes his name to the fact that you can ask him about any train departure or arrival in the past, and he will spit out the exact timings. Mr Antonio Correa-Afonso, a wonderful man in his eighties, who lived with his wife, Marina, around the corner from us and hailed from one of the old influential families of Benaulim, took pride in Benaulim's reputation: 'The people of Moira are just plain mad. But the Banalcars (people of Benaulim) would like to believe that their eccentricity is a unique characteristic of their genius.'

---

1 See Fr Nascimento Mascarenha, 'What Are Goa's Villages Famous For?' (www.saligaoserenade.com).

Our village of eccentrics has been the cradle of many influential people. During the Portuguese era, it produced judges, lawyers, educationists, doctors, even two bishops. Another was Fancu, a genius of Western classical music, who composed waltzes and mandos. And not to forget Armia de Se, born in 1880, who was known for being the first woman in Goa to break the 'tradition' of girls staying at home: she obtained a secondary education at a time when this was indeed revolutionary. Another remarkable woman was Propercia Correa-Afonso de Figueiredo, a woman born in the nineteenth century, who never went to a formal school, but was believed to be highly educated, completely self-taught, and became a noted authority on ancient Indian history and Goan folklore. She was part of the famous Correa-Afonso clan and her cheerful grand-niece Deepa is our house doctor in case of an emergency. The internationally acclaimed architect Charles Correa, who lives in Bombay, also hails from this family. I met him once at a dinner party thrown by the celebrated photographer Dayanita Singh at her house in Saligao, where one often meets interesting people. Charles Correa not only creates amazing buildings, but also addresses social issues, such as low-income housing and urban planning, and has been deeply involved in the formulation of the Regional Plan 2021 for Goa.[2]

Apart from its well-known families, there are many unknown heroes in my village. One of them is Shiva, a forty-two-year-old

---

2 The Regional Plan 2011 threatened to change orchards, agricultural land, forests, etc. into settlement areas for construction. Due to pressure from the Goan citizen movement, a new plan is in the process of being designed with the support of eminent architects such as Dean de Cruz and Charles Correa, with a fresh blueprint to preserve Goa's eco-sensitive areas. The acceptance of the new Regional Plan is still awaited.

man, originally from Hola-Alur in Karnataka, who is a Benaulim institution. He is a man rejected or at best ignored by the villagers, especially the young guys on their motorcycles who hang around at the main crossroads wasting their lives, while Shiva at least tries to earn a decent living. Shiva has lived in Goa for the past twenty-six years and describes himself as 'a cheap dog, easy to impress and easy to please'. Asked why he would say this about himself, he answered, 'I take what is offered to me.' And indeed, he has the fine nose of a dog when it comes to foreign tourists. I would bet that any foreigner who stays longer than a few days in Benaulim will run into Shiva. One sees him on the beach where he sells postcards with stamps, organizes train and bus tickets, invites tourists to his home and generally chats them up, while his wife teaches them to cook a few Goan dishes. Shiva organizes birdwatching tours, sells donated second-hand books after reading most of them himself, collects clothes and other items from foreigners who go back home and distributes them among his family members and needy people, collects plastic bottles, rents out bicycles—the list goes on. 'I have many zero-expense ideas,' Shiva says.

'You know,' he continues, 'before I came to Goa, I never had more than one meal a day. I did not even possess two shirts or a pair of sandals.' Constantly struggling to make a living out of tourists so that he can send his three kids to school, he nevertheless carries bundles of ten-rupee notes in his pockets, which he hands out to the homeless and sick or old people in need. He shares at least fifty rupees a day from his income with people whose fate could easily have been his own. Quoting Anne Frank, he says, 'There is no wrong time to do the right thing.'

Talking to him, one soon realizes that he has an amazing memory, which, however, does not really distinguish between the important and the unimportant. His greatest gift is his ability to speak foreign languages, none of which was formally taught to him. He speaks seven foreign languages fluently and another eight well, and this does not include languages where he can do some basic chit-chatting and small talk. Shiva knows languages as obscure as Welsh and Slovenian. His 'island of ability', which is truly startling, is his entry point when he sees a new 'foreign face' in Benaulim, because Shiva will not waste a minute before talking to you in your language. He feels extremely happy when he can speak to someone in their own language, and when sad, he sings in French. When a friend of mine first bumped into him, he thought he was caught in some 'hidden-camera scene', because Shiva, as soon as he had figured out that my friend came from Ireland, started speaking to him in Gaelic. This friend identified Shiva's linguistic skills as Savant syndrome, a rare gift of a prodigious memory in fields such as languages and music. 'He spoke Irish much better than I do,' he recalled in awe. Shiva listens to the radio station Deutsche Welle to polish his German and reads every book that comes his way, his favourite being dictionaries. He knows almost all the postal codes of England, Scotland and Ireland and loves to quote all kinds of celebrities from poets to politicians, whether it is Willie Brandt or Barack Obama. He sings Marlene Dietrich songs and knows all about the German football club Schalke 04.

Shiva ran away at fifteen from an alcoholic, though talented, father who wrote plays, but that never gave him enough of an income to feed his family. When he came to Goa, Shiva knew immediately that this was where he wanted to be. He manages in the most creative ways to make his living, and always has a smile on his face when he waves to me from his bicycle.

Aside from its characters, there are other things that set Benaulim apart—the sounds one hears here, for instance. Most of the houses have a garden with some palm trees and fruit trees, and a few pigs and chickens. At dusk, I hear a chorus of villagers calling *yau-yau-yau* (or *ge-yau, ge-yau, ge-yau*), meaning come, come, come, to coax their pigs home. That's followed by another chorus of *ba-ba-ba,* as the chickens are called home to roost. My neighbour, despite his many ba-ba-bas, doesn't have much success getting his chickens into the henhouse at night. They sit on the lower branches of the guava tree or on the parapet of the rear wall dividing our properties. Sometimes we see him late at night looking for them with a flashlight, ba-baing away, until he finally loses patience and gets them down with a stick. Once in a while, one of his chickens decides to visit our garden, but soon realizes that this is a bad idea, since it gets chased by my dogs, who in turn, are chased by me.

We have two cats and two dogs, and I have long wanted to add two more family pets—a grey parrot (my childhood dream, since they are very smart and learn to speak easily) and a pet pig that could sleep on the veranda and eat leftovers and potato peels. I pictured myself yodelling *yau-yau-yau* every evening as dusk fell, and telling my friends, 'There goes your vindaloo,' before serving them a vegetarian meal. Pigs, however, have served more purposes than just vindaloo in Goa—the pig-loo was the only available toilet in Goa before flush toilets and septic tanks arrived on the scene. The pig-loo was where a Goan's rejects would land up, sliding into a trench at the back of the toilet where the pig would roam around and act as a mobile waste-disposal unit (put you off your vindaloo and sorpotel?). After eating this gourmet breakfast, the pig would find a pool of stagnant water heated by the sun and settle down for a nice jacuzzi.[3] It is these associations that come to my husband's mind when thinking of pigs. And since I did not want him or Kailash to move out, and had learned that pigs eat flowers and banana trees, I gave up the idea of convincing Sudhir to gift me a pet pig.

Benaulim, a sleepy fishing community just ten years ago, is changing rapidly. It is still a beautiful place, despite the mushrooming of construction sites. Shops, hotels and beauty salons are finding their way into the village; even a Baskin-Robbins ice-cream parlour opened a few seasons ago. This kind of 'development' seems to be the destiny of the whole Goan coastal belt. It scares me to imagine that Benaulim might resemble Calangute, Anjuna or Baga in another ten years; peaceful hamlets of fisherfolk till a generation ago, that have become dirty, noisy, open bazaars today—an Ibiza or Costa del Sol of India—dominated by cheating vendors and 'white trash', as I call a certain breed of tourists that seems to be the bane of every country. They are completely uninterested in the culture of the community or the country they are visiting; they don't really care whether they are flying to the Dominican Republic or India, as long as there is a sunny beach and enough beer around, the first bottles emptied at breakfast. So far, Benaulim has been frequented predominantly by more grounded tourists—young backpackers and Indian families—and I hope we will be spared the 'Baga syndrome'. But with each passing year I wonder if my optimism has any basis in reality. In truth, I do fear that the quiet charms of my village will soon be history.

With new opportunities and quick money from the tourism

---

3 See Claude Alvares, *Fish Curry and Rice* (Mapusa: Goa Foundation, 2002), p. 323.

industry, the old professions of Benaulim—fishing, agriculture, animal husbandry and carpentry—are struggling to survive. Our village has traditionally been a hub of carpenters. A few generations ago, they were well known for carving the most exquisite furniture out of rosewood, which can still be seen in the old aristocratic houses of Goa, and is often referred to as 'black wood', since the wood is very dark. Today, they no longer carve rosewood. They only make cheap furniture, displayed and sold at fairs during the major religious festivals. Still, the many carpenters in Benaulim try to eke out a living; there are three in our neighbourhood alone. Their sons, much better educated, look for less hard and better-paid professions, and are unwilling to step into their fathers' shoes. And who can blame them?

Many traditional village professions will die out or change into something else within the next two generations. Take, for example, the local fishermen in their wooden catamarans: they have switched over to dolphin-watching and motorboats for tourists. Toddy tappers, basket weavers, village bakers and many others now find it difficult to feed a family, what with rising prices and the changing demands of modern life. As Teotonio R. de Souza writes in his book *Goa To Me*, in the past, 'Every village had a certain number of servants whose non-agricultural services were essential for the economic self-sufficiency of a village, such as the carpenter (*thovoi*), blacksmith (*vinani*), washerman (*dhobi*), potter (*kumbhar*), barber (*malo*), basket weaver (*mahar*), cobbler (*chamar*), boatman (*tari*). These services were directly associated with the agricultural needs of a village.'[4] The economic interdependence of different professions within a

---

4   Teotonio R. de Souza, *Goa To Me* (New Delhi: Concept, 1994), p. 53.

community, all contributing their bit to enable a village to function and prosper, is now a thing of the past and a basket weaver or cobbler can no longer earn a sufficient income in this new world with its new professions and temptations. Their children grow up with Facebook and mobile phones and have different values and ambitions. Those who do not leave Goa to work in the Gulf countries dream of running beach shacks and bars; they rent out rooms to tourists in their homes or get involved in the taxi business. Many feel that tourism alone will butter their bread. Even very successful family businesses that earn well and are greatly in demand for their old-fashioned ways of delivering quality, like the Jila bakery in Ambora, might die out. Reginaldo Antao of the Jila bakery, who has bagged many awards, including the prestigious Best Bakery Award for his delicious biscuits and cakes (the only place I shop for biscuits ever since I discovered this family-run establishment), says that his children have other plans—they have no intention of getting up at four in the morning to make dough and light the wood-fired oven.

Some professions, such as coconut plucking, will die out even faster, unless a new generation is trained. In our own garden, around 800 coconuts have to be cut every three months and picked up by a local trader who lives in our neighbourhood. I am always surprised by the sheer number of coconuts our palm trees produce even without fertilizer. In the good old days when the catch of fish used to be plentiful, the excess catch used to be dumped in the coconut groves as fertilizer. It must have smelt terrible, but the swaying palms responded to their fishy feed with an abundant yield. Our coconut trees are less demanding. As long as they are watered regularly, they are satisfied with the ash of burnt leaves. It is quite a spectacle to watch the coconut pluckers climb up the tree with just a coir rope, locally called *summ*, stretched between their feet and a *koyto* knife held between their teeth. They seem to climb with incredible ease (I did not manage to clamber up even one metre when I tried) and though accidents probably happen, I have never heard of one. The pluckers I have met in the ten years of living in Benaulim are invariably uneducated and of middle age or older. They are in such demand that they can do a lousy job and still quote any price. In Kerala, which has the same problem, people have started to train monkeys to do the job. I wouldn't mind a pet monkey harvesting our trees since walking beneath overripe bunches of coconuts can be seriously hazardous. I'm only half joking when I tell Germans planning to visit us (known for their passion for insurance policies) that they better get insured against injuries from coconuts.

If one ignores the haphazard construction boom and the growing piles of plastic garbage, one can still delude oneself by painting an idyllic picture of village life in Goa: slim wooden catamarans returning to shore early in the morning with buckets full of sardines; women chatting and singing while planting rice; water buffaloes wallowing happily in shallow waterbodies; groups of fishermen mending their nets, salting and drying the unsold fish on the sun-warmed asphalt; old people sitting in front of their houses reading newspapers or taking care of their grandchildren; rural communities living in harmony with each other and with nature and so on and so forth. However, beneath the surface, the realities of day-to-day village life are quite different. The more I observe village life in Benaulim, the more these fantasies of a rural idyll are shattered. Take, for example, my neighbour: over the months, I watched him drink himself to death. His son regularly beat him up and he would retaliate by accusing the son of sleeping with his own mother. With all the respect that I have for Mahatma Gandhi, I cannot agree with his idealization of village life. Miss Marple, Agatha Christie's famous amateur detective, was nearer the truth when she maintained that even the most picturesque and outwardly tranquil village communities have dark and evil undercurrents. Life in Benaulim, as I have observed and experienced it, is as much fuelled by jealousy, corruption and deceit as it is in any metropolis. Alcoholism and domestic violence are rampant. And from the political class and the elite to the *aam admi,* it is common practice to misuse connections, run down one's neighbours and refuse to engage in any activity for the benefit of the entire community.

The rapid change in coastal Goa, though it comes at a heavy price, is not all bad, of course—most families benefit in significant ways and those lamenting that Goa is going to the pits would certainly not change their new lifestyle to go back to the life of their grandparents, unless they belong to the elite families of the former colonialists with all their privileges. However, in today's asymmetric society, where wealth is more than ever before unevenly divided among the 'haves' and the 'have-nots' who constantly struggle to make a living, 'making a fast buck' can become the guiding mantra of life. Indeed, in Goa, 'making a fast buck' is increasingly becoming the norm without even the slightest moral remorse. Goan ministers are not exactly shining examples of integrity and their behaviour and moral standards seem to have had a trickle-down effect, giving others the green light to feather their nests in whatever way they can. Whether it is the carpenter who buys cheap wood but charges for expensive wood; the worker who turns up drunk and does a shoddy job but charges triple the going rate; the taxi driver or shopkeeper blithely cheating visitors who do not know the local prices—you will find it all here. This attitude, often carefully hidden at least as long as that person still hopes to get something out of you, is something one shouldn't take personally. More painful, however, is the price they pay for such an ethic: the loss of integrity and of a sense of pride in what they do or produce. Whether a smart banker, a creative artist or an illiterate mason, the work one is skilled in can be a source of deep satisfaction if one gives one's best, if one treats one's work (as much as the other person) with honesty and respect. So many in Goa, especially in its famed beach belt, have unfortunately lost that.

However, despite slowly losing the glue that binds its society, my village has many attractive features. Many of my fellow villagers are unfailingly helpful and courteous and have strong personal values, such as my neighbours Tina and John; or Cecilia, who lives close by and helps with the daily chores in my house. Their lives are carefully folded into a reality that seems far removed from the hustlers who hang around beach tourists and from the techno–trance pool parties. Their lives revolve around family, neighbours and the church. They are deeply traditional, have a sense of honour and follow a strong moral code. Some of them work very hard and do well, some struggle, others prefer to do nothing. For those who do nothing, their basic needs are covered with a roof over their head, a few pigs and chicken and some fruit and coconut trees, so their attitude seems to be, why work unnecessarily? One of my neighbours, self-employed and always short of money, was asked to do a small job at our house involving the shifting of a boiler. This required a little effort, but was well paid, since the boiler to be removed was hidden in an awkward corner under the elevated water tank. He climbed the ladder and looked at it. 'Why don't you leave it there? No harm!' he said. 'No, no,' I responded, since we had a solar panel to heat our water and did not need a boiler, 'it will just go to waste, please take it down so we can give it to someone who can make use of it.' He nodded, came down the ladder and said he would be back in the afternoon. He never showed up again.

This lack of interest in work, even if well paid, may also be a lack of interest in helping outsiders like us, who do not belong to the community. Our life might be as alien to him as his is to us. It might be a demonstration of shrugging us off as outsiders, or it could simply be indifference and peasant stubbornness. I must admit that I have a sneaking admiration for the fact that the day-to-day life of many villagers is not yet dictated by time and money alone. They have their own logic that often rattles one's own certainties.

Having lived among the Banalcars for quite some time now, are we part of their community? We are not. Partly, I think, because of our lack of participation in their religious rituals, partly because we have chosen to keep a distance, partly because the villagers have chosen to keep their distance. I suppose one could ask the same question of Indians who have chosen to live in a small corner of Germany—I wonder if they feel they have been accepted as part of that community.

And are we happy here? Yes, we are. We feel at home, we have created our island of peace and we have been made to feel welcome in a community that is, on the whole, remarkably tolerant and accepting of those from other cultures and ways of life.

5

Where the Arrow Struck

Any observation about Goan village life is incomplete without an exploration of Goa's religious history and its undercurrents, since the church is such a dominating factor in the coastal belt. Though Catholics make up less than a third of Goa's population, the vast majority of Benaulim's population is Roman Catholic (the more one moves inland, the more Hindu the villages become). Benaulim, which today includes the villages of Cana and Adsulim, is located in the *taluka* of Salcete, which got its name from the Sanskrit word *sassat*, meaning sixty-six (villages) or maybe, as Teotonio R. de Souza claims, from *shastha*, referring to the ocean, which played such an important role in the economy of its early settlers.[1] Salcete belongs to the old conquests of the Portuguese, the *Velhas Conquistas*, occupied in the early years of Portuguese colonialism, dominated and deeply moulded by the Jesuits. It is the only Catholic-majority (around 70 per cent of the population) taluka in Goa. The first parish priest of Benaulim was the Jesuit Pero Berno, who came from Ascona in Italy. He, along with other Jesuits, was murdered in 1583 by angry villagers of nearby Cuncolim, when he arrived there to survey the place with the intention of building a church.

The Jesuits were in Goa between 1542 and 1759 till the expulsion of their order (they were the first of the orders to be

---

1 Teotonio R. de Souza, *Goa To Me* (New Delhi: Concept, 1994), p. 32.

suppressed, but eventually, by 1835, all religious orders had to leave Goa and it took the Jesuits almost 200 years to return to Goa).[2] With the expulsion of the Jesuits, education standards plummeted and Salcete lost its best teachers. The Jesuits contributed in many ways to Goan life, including agricultural innovations, but they were fanatical in their commitment to convert the Indian 'heathens'. Salcete suffered terribly under the Inquisition, which also saw the destruction of its Hindu temples. The edict of 1540 gave the Portuguese viceroy authority to destroy any Hindu temple within an area under Portuguese control and by the end of the sixteenth century, the destruction and suppression of other faiths was in full swing. Benaulim used to have eight temples, as recorded in the *Foral Velho de 1567*.[3] None of the old structures survived the Inquisition.

It is believed that the main church in Benaulim, named after St John the Baptist—an impressive building founded in 1581—was originally constructed at the site of a temple for Benespur or Banespor, the Lord of the Arrow, close to the shore. It was shifted in 1596 to its present site on the Monte Benaulim, a low hill far removed from the village centre. The interior of St John the Baptist Church is one of the finest examples of the rococo style and is worth a visit. There is a beautiful story woven around the deity Benespur, whose temple had to give way to the Benaulim church. According to Hindu mythology, Goa and the Konkan

---

2 As pointed out by Teotonio de Souza, the suppression was largely motivated by the growing bankruptcy of the Portuguese state and the eagerness of its political leaders to exploit the resentment of the people regarding the prosperity of religious institutions. See ibid. pp. 60, 104.

3 Roque Muniz, 'Opusculo Historiques'. *Bannauli* (Sanquelim: Konkani Seva Kendra, 1992), pp. 38–9.

coastal region were created by Parashurama, the sixth incarnation of Lord Vishnu, by shooting an arrow into the sea. In order to find a sanctified piece of land to perform his fire sacrifices, Parashurama shot his arrow into the ocean and commanded the sea to retreat to the point at which the arrow had fallen. The sea retreated and the Konkan coast was formed. The god then settled ninety-six Brahmin families on the reclaimed land. According to this popular legend, Benaulim derived its name from Bannavli, the place where Parashurama's arrow had struck the ground.[4]

Claiming that there is evidence of marine fossil findings, geologists today say that the legend of the receding waters may have arisen from a geological process around 12000 BC, when submerged land was elevated as a result of violent tectonic movements. And one does indeed find marine fossil deposits in places such as Chicalim (in the taluka of Mormugao) and Siridao (a village near Bambolim).

Possibly, every tourist coming to our village will hear the story of Parashurama shooting his arrow. At least, this was the conversation I got into when the taxi driver brought us to our village for the first time and I have had to listen to it many, many times over the years. Some locals say the arrow fell into the 'Lake of the Lotus' called Komllam Tollem, which I pass often on my way to the fish and fruit market in Margao. Locals believe that this is the reason it has thousands of fragrant lotus blossoms. Though Lord Benespur did not survive the razing of his temple when the Inquisition roared into Salcete, oral history has kept his myth alive.

Whenever I go to Vaddo beach to walk my dog at sunset, I pass

---

4 In a less popular version, Benaulim got its name from *Vann-halli*, the forest-covered village.

another prominent church, the Trinity Church, closer to the centre of Benaulim. It is believed that it too stands on the site of a temple called Samtery, possibly referring to the local mother goddess Santeri, the Goddess of the Anthill. There is another temple near our house, which, according to folklore, was destroyed, bringing in its wake a curse on the site where it once stood. The villagers tell me the old pillars of that temple are still buried in a nearby pond, and maintain that anyone coming close to those pillars will fall dangerously ill. When I told Sudhir about my discovery of the destroyed, accursed temple, he commented, 'Rumours kept alive around the curse indicate that the local population, most probably watching quietly in fear, must have had a guilty conscience for allowing the temples to get destroyed.'

The Inquisition and the destruction of temples in Goa were traumatic events, never fully processed by its people. Reports of Jesuits who witnessed the destruction within Salcete give an idea of the impact it must have had at the time: 'Some were burnt down, others were heaped as garbage, and still others were razed to the ground. Nearly 280 of these were big ones and some of them were sumptuous and of exceedingly fine workmanship.' [5] The man behind the brutal destruction of hundreds of temples in our area was the infamous Diogo Rodrigues, who was feared as 'O do Forte', the man of the fort, since he held a powerful position as captain of the Jesuit Seminary of Rachol, a beautiful and very special place that I have visited several times. The Rachol seminary, where the Catholic clergy is trained even today, has a superb library and enough antique furniture, relics and paintings

---

5 *Documenta Indica*, VII, p. 391, cited in Teotonio R. de Souza, *Goa To Me*, p. 94.

to furnish a whole village. Not far from the seminary, in the Rachol Parish Church, located near the Zuari river, a memorial slab reminds visitors of the terrifying deeds of Diogo Rodrigues, who was buried in the church in 1577. With the destruction of the temples, Hindu centres of learning and teaching were destroyed as well, and centuries of knowledge and culture were wiped out. However, whenever possible, local Hindus brought the remains of their destroyed temples to safety in a neighbouring territory and continued to worship their gods, risking their lives by secretly crossing the border into areas out of reach of the Portuguese. Many of those who got caught were tried by the tribunals of the Inquisition. They were often brutally interrogated and tortured, flogged or slowly dismembered.

Not a single temple of Salcete survived the Inquisition, which lasted in Goa till 1812. The construction of today's only existing Hindu temple in Benaulim took place as late as 1921. It is an ugly and inconspicuous concrete building dedicated to the Goddess Lakshmi and when passing by, I have never seen a soul on its premises.

Our village is today enriched with seven churches and chapels, most of them probably standing where temples once stood. All of them are crowded for Sunday Mass, some of them are even full for a Mass on weekdays. I see the faithful of my neighbourhood walk to the morning sermon as I pass the Patricinio Chapel on the way to my yoga class. In a great mood after an hour of stretching and breathing, I sometimes hear their hymns. I love the singing. And I love that the villagers put on their best clothes to go to Mass, especially on feast days. The Patricinio Chapel was built in 1805 and has a beautiful whitewashed facade with the priest's house right next to it. I have attended sermons there twice: once, when my neighbour died and another time, when visiting friends from Germany wanted to 'experience' a Goan midnight Mass at Christmas, which lasted till 2 a.m.

Benaulim, I was told, is the only village on Goa's south coast that is dominated by people of Brahmin origin. Perhaps Brahmin settlers felt attracted to the village because of the Parashurama myth, which claims that Vishnu settled the first ninety-six Brahmin families here. It is thus not surprising that our village is also known as Bamangaon or Brahmingaon, the village of Brahmins. Other than in places such as Chandor, Benaulim has no settlements of the Kunbi and Gauda tribal communities, which again could be an indicator that it was a powerful Brahmin centre before the Portuguese arrived. Being tribal people—in the past, they were usually landless labourers—the Kunbis and Gaudas were considered as polluters of the sanctified high-caste village. Their absence here reflects the rigid caste boundaries in Hinduism.

Despite the Portuguese endeavour to diminish the caste system, it exists today to a certain extent even among Goa's Catholics. It is visible, for example, in matrimonial advertisements in local newspapers, where a groom looks for a fair-skinned 'Christian Brahmin' bride. The importance of caste for Goan Catholics is reflected also in a decree by Pope Gregory XV in 1623, stating that 'Brahmins converted to Catholicism might wear their sacred cord and caste marks, provided these were blessed by a Catholic Priest'.[6] The priests were well aware that they would be unable to convert the masses without converting the Brahmin elite, who, as landlords, had tremendous influence on the village folk. Thus

---

6 Manohar Malgonkar, *Inside Goa* (Bardez: Architecture Autonomous, 2004, 1982), p. 77.

they had to accept caste in Goan Catholicism. Sudhir's comment on Pope Gregory XV's decree sums up its implications most succinctly: 'This shows that for Hindus it was more important to keep their caste than to keep their gods.'

Despite the presence of caste in Goan Catholicism, the sense of equality among people is much stronger in Christian Goa than in many other parts of India and for that at least the Portuguese have to be thanked. When our Hindu housekeeper Kailash and his family moved with us to Goa, he was pleasantly surprised to find how differently he was treated in Benaulim compared to Delhi and other places in India, where he often suffered humiliation.

Despite the changes that are affecting society in rural Goa, religion still has a strong hold on village life. Natives of Benaulim believe their village is especially blessed, because the Patron of Missionaries, Father Joseph Vaz, was born here, around the corner from my house, 350 years before we moved here. He is regarded as the most famous son of our village because when in 1995 he was beatified by Pope John Paul II, he became the only Goan to hold that distinction. Father Vaz played a prominent role in the struggle of the Goan clergy to get accepted to higher positions that were only open to European priests. Though the first Goan priest was ordained as early as 1558, Goans—even the most talented— were not allowed to move up in the ecclesiastical hierarchy within Portuguese territory. With a number of other priests, Father Vaz became a leading member of the St Philip Neri's Oratorians, a society of Catholic priests and lay brothers bound together by no formal vows but only by the bond of charity. This step also marked his protest against the racism of the Catholic Church. It is ironic, however, that Father Vaz, a Gaud Saraswat Brahmin, was as much a 'child of his time' as the Portuguese, since he permitted only Brahmins to hold positions in the new congregation! The struggle to end the racism of the Portuguese church took a long time—the first native-born Archbishop of Goa was appointed as late as 1978.

Today, perhaps out of embarrassment for its history of racism, the Catholic Church prefers to emphasize Father Vaz's achievements as a missionary in Ceylon (now Sri Lanka), where he worked for twenty-four years, 'risking his life to spread the message of the Lord in the land of the heretics', as the Church puts it. In church pamphlets to honour his birthday, his rebellious activities are not mentioned. His house—or rather, the cross and statue of him in front of it—is still a place of worship, where villagers come every day to light candles and offer flowers. One afternoon, out of curiosity, I went to the house where he was born, to see if any of his descendants were still living there. Antonio, an elderly gentleman who lives there now, told me that Father Vaz's descendants had sold the house two generations ago and moved away from the village. He has no idea where they might be now.

Today, there is no trace of the Hindu Brahmin village that Benaulim used to be five centuries ago. I sometimes wander its streets and wonder how Goan villages in the coastal belt, now dominated by the Catholic culture, would look if the Portuguese had never conquered Goa. No churches, no pigs; saris instead of dresses; maybe not even tomatoes, potatoes and chillies, since these vegetables, introduced by the Portuguese (as so many other plants), took a very long time to be accepted into Hindu cooking. And no grand houses built by the former elite of the Portuguese colonial government, such as the magnificent mansions of Chandor, Loutolim and so many other villages which are such an enchanting feature of Goa's landscape.

6

Houses of Chandor, Houses of Loutolim

'Goa was not liberated, my dear, it was invaded by the Indian army!' This was my introduction to eighty-one-year-old Dona Maria Lourdes Figueiredo-Albuquerque from Loutolim, a formidable grande dame who has fascinating stories to tell about her life and family. The views of Maria de Lourdes, a member of a family that belonged to Goa's ruling class, are echoed by many others in Goa, even average middle-class folk. One such is Brian Bones, an Afro-haired musician whom we sometimes run into at a bar in Benaulim, where he hangs out to sing karaoke in the off season, when time is ample and engagements rare. The manner in which the Portuguese rule ended is a debate that's still alive among Goans. As a man with the impressive name of Gaganappa Hassan Ali Nagarjuna Tennyson India (G.H.A.N.T.I. for short), pithily put it: 'Some called it liberation, some still call it an invasion, so, you guys still could not reconcile if you were free or enslaved.'[1]

The Indian army marched into Goa on 19 December 1961, chasing the Portuguese away after 451 years of colonialism, in an operation code-named 'Operation Vijay'. At that time, it was not universally seen as a 'liberation' of Goa, with some United

---

1 See Oscar Rebello, 'G.H.A.N.T.I.', in *Herald*, 13 March 2011 (http://goa365.blogspot.com/2011/03/heraldo-1332011-published.html).

Nations member countries proposing a resolution condemning the invasion which, however, was vetoed by the then USSR.

For the old landed gentry of Goa, the shock of 'liberation' saw the end of a way of life. There is, even today, a grudge about the losses these old families had to bear. Some of their members even talk of 'daylight robbery' fifty years after the Portuguese were forced to leave and their privileges taken from them. The land reforms of 1962 forced such families to give up land that they had leased out to tenants, depriving them of their substantial agricultural revenues and income. *Goa Indica*, a liberation for the masses, meant sudden social insignificance and economic insecurity for the former ruling class. For them (to borrow Sudhir's phrase), 'It was much more painful to have fallen from the top, than never to have risen at all.'

The families affected by the land reforms claimed that this was mainly the newly formed government's way of gaining popularity and winning the votes of the *aam admi*. Be that as it may, Goan voters went to the polls in a referendum and voted overwhelmingly to become an autonomous, centrally administered territory of India. Only as late as 1987 did Goa become a fully fledged state of India.

When I entered the beautiful mansion of Mrs Maria de Lourdes (which is what I call her, since her last name is unpronounceable for my German tongue) for the first time, it felt like stepping into a time warp. A grand staircase swept up to the front door, flanked by lush lawns and flowering shrubs. Nothing seemed to have changed for the past century and a half. I experienced similar feelings of having entered a time capsule when I visited the impressive Menezes-Braganza mansion in Chandor and the Fernandes Heritage Inn, also in Chandor. In the house of the

Mirandas, a beautiful fortress in Loutolim with exquisite mosaic flooring in patterns of birds and dogs, none of the original furniture remains, but the old chapel allows one to imagine the beauty and grandeur of the house in the old days.

Mrs Maria de Lourdes's old retainer led me into the salon through a library furnished with an ornate desk and shelves lined with leather-bound books. The house still has its original tiled and wooden floors, the salon is decorated with baroque carved rosewood furniture, lace tablecloths, Chinese porcelain of different eras and styles on the walls and tables, and crystal chandeliers. The salon doors open to a beautiful view of paddy fields with a coconut grove lining the horizon. Mrs Maria de Lourdes showed me around her sprawling house, talking animatedly about the weddings, dances and great banquets that were held there. The library, ballroom, salon and dining hall, the private chapel within the mansion, collections of delicate porcelain, a profusion of carved rosewood and oyster-shell windows letting in a lovely translucent light—all these are typical features of these mansions, mirroring the life of the Portuguese–Goan elite of the nineteenth century whose descendants, such as the Mirandas, Braganzas, de Silvas, Deshprabhus and Figueiredo-Albuquerques, take pride in preserving the legacy of their ancestors.

When did the Goan elite start building these great houses and adopting this lavish lifestyle? By the mid-eighteenth century, Christians in Goa felt much more settled and united as a social group; their wealth was growing rapidly, thanks to the richness of the land, the growth of locally based trade and Portugal's new prosperity, much of it fuelled by Brazilian gold that also flowed into Goa. And that is when the great family estates of Goa began to be established. The Goan landowners were quick to develop a taste for Portuguese-style rococo elegance which they grafted on to their domestic architecture, their clothes, music and food.[2] The walls of the Figueiredo-Albuquerque mansion are lined with oil paintings of family members, a particularly striking one being a portrait of Mrs Maria de Lourdes's beautiful great-grandmother, posing in a Mando dress. Goans loved (and still love) to dance and during Portuguese times developed a dance, the Mando, which is connected to a specific, dark and romantic style of music. The Mando was considered one of the last aristocratic dance forms.

Mrs Maria de Lourdes also pointed out to me furniture and porcelain from all over the world, including hand-painted Chinese crockery sets with bespoke designs done just for the family.

She is an outspoken lady—entertaining, witty and a great raconteur, and in her eventful life she has even been a member of the Portuguese Parliament. High tea or lunch at her home is a memorable experience: her food, all home cooked, is outstanding and served with great elegance. She keeps herself fit, energetic and engaged, she informed me in her smoky voice, through 'exercise and reading'.

The Figueiredo family has been very influential in Goa's history and politics, having produced many doctors, lawyers and judges. Mrs Maria de Lourdes, with her aristocratic bearing, natural self-confidence and dignity, sees it as her duty to maintain the house and keep its legacy alive. 'This house is part of Goa's cultural heritage and it needs to be open to the public,' she declares. After her sister's death in 2008, the house, in collaboration with the Xavier Centre of Historical Research, has been converted into a vibrant living museum that evokes a vanished era. With enough notice,

2 See Maurice Hall, *Window on Goa* (London: Quiller Press, 1992), p. 32.

she even accepts bookings from visiting groups and hosts them for an elaborate meal. The negligence of the Goa government and its ministers towards the old mansions is regrettable. There are many such buildings all over Goa, some of them well known, such as the huge Deshprabhu mansion in Pernem or the home of the de Silvas in Margao. Others are quietly tucked away between coconut groves and paddy fields, in varied states of disrepair. But the Goa government does nothing to preserve this unique cultural heritage. The wake-up call, if it comes at all, might come too late, since the structures are crumbling and few among the younger generation are willing to make the sacrifices necessary to restore a house that scarcely gives them any income.

An exception is the young Goan couple Ruben and Celia Vasco da Gama, who leased the Palácio do Deão for sixty years from the church. Ruben and Celia, both hailing from prestigious Goan families, wanted a spacious, peaceful place to raise their children and at the same time make a living. A hidden jewel in the otherwise overbuilt small-town atmosphere of Quepem, the Palácio do Deão is located on the banks of the Kushavati, a clear-blue wild river in which I once spotted a crocodile. There is an interesting story around this 200-year-old palace. It was built by the Portuguese nobleman and dean of the Church, Deão Jose Paulo, who arrived in Goa in 1779. The Palácio faces the Church of Quepem and, as an inscription in the churchyard proclaims, the Deão financed half the town out of his own pocket, including the church. The Deão was known as the 'barefooted friar' and while building Quepem, which was then a forested area, he constructed two columns at the entrance of the town and decreed that any criminal entering Quepem beyond those columns and willing to work could rehabilitate himself there.

Another story is connected to his death. He died in January 1835 and willed that his Palácio, which he modestly called his farmhouse, would be inherited by his soul. There is a deep-rooted superstition in the Goan mind connected to properties known as *pensavnchem bhat*, properties that are willed with the condition that the deceased souls must be prayed for regularly. That way, the church earned a lot of donations from people trying to rid themselves of the Masses that were 'owed' to the deceased owners of the houses they were living in. In the past, Goans often refused to buy or move into properties known as pensavnchem bhat; even the fruit in the gardens of such properties was not plucked but left to rot. Today, when property prices are shooting through the roof, no one seems to care too much any longer, but in earlier times, buyers often asked for certificates stating that the property was without *pensao*—the promise to offer repose to the soul of the former owner. There is a general fear even today that people who buy such properties don't prosper.[3] The soul of Deão Jose Paulo, however, seems to be a benevolent one, since Celia and Ruben have had a lot of luck with their big project—renovating the mansion, finding furniture of the right period and so on. They only realized what they had got themselves into after they leased the Palácio from the *cabido*. When offered to Ruben and Celia, it was in a completely derelict state. The couple renovated it with their own savings and a lot of love and care. Over the past few years they have recreated the gardens to look the way they used to in the old days and have furnished all rooms with eighteenth-century antiques. If booked in advance, they offer

---

3 See Alexandre Moniz Barbosa, 'Pensao: A Tradition Wrapped in Myth', in *Times of India*, 2 November 2009, p. 4.

Indo-Portuguese cuisine to guests, all cooked by Celia, who has revived traditional Goan recipes. I have dined at Palácio do Deão many times and it has always been a wonderful experience.

However, organizing lunches and dinners for tourists and strangers, as Ruben and Celia do in order to earn an income, is not something that all families who have opened their heritage homes to visitors are prepared to undertake. Some try to balance expenses by allowing film crews to camp in their homes for weeks or even months. Take, for example, the Braganzas' house in Chandor or the magnificent ancestral home of the famous cartoonist Mario Miranda in Loutolim, located not too far from the house of his childhood friend, Mrs Maria de Lourdes. The acclaimed director Shyam Benegal, a friend of Mario's, shot the Hindi film *Trikaal* (Past, Present, Future), a story set in Christian Goa, there (I wonder why Goan characters in Bollywood movies are always Christians, when Christians are a 30 per cent minority within Goa?). Mario's wife, Habiba, smiled wryly as she recalled the film shoot: 'It was a disaster! Thirty people marching in and out, using the toilet and the kitchen. And instead of renovating the house as promised, they only renovated the corners they needed for the shooting.' Nevertheless, thanks to *Trikaal*, the Mirandas were able to restore their chapel to its old glory. The two-storeyed Miranda house was one of the grandest Goan houses in the times of *Goa Portuguesa*. For centuries, the family held high positions in the colonial administration and also produced two of its most powerful judges. They were generously rewarded for their loyalty. In the nineteenth century, the then head of the Miranda family was knighted by the Portuguese, who bestowed on them a family crest which still adorns the main entrance.

Habiba recounts that this honour was given to the family after

Constancio Miranda, the administrator of Ponda district at that time, laid a trap and shot dead the bandit Kustoba Rane, who had come to secretly visit his lover in Loutolim. Other sources, however, say he was killed in Collem, betrayed by his mistress, a *bhavin* or temple maid of that village.[4]

The Rane clan of Sattari taluka had launched over a dozen rebellions against the Portuguese between 1740 and 1912, spreading terror among the rich whose houses they robbed regularly. However, for the common man, the poor and the underclass, Kustoba Rane was a hero—a composite of Robin Hood and Rambo, as the famous Goan writer Manohar Malgonkar, who gave Goa its most romantic folk tales and its most spirited campfire songs, put it.[5] The Goan artist Subodh Kerkar told me the story of how he once met an aged shepherd on one of his walks. While talking about politics, it transpired that the old man had no clue the Portuguese had ever conquered Goa! He believed the Ranes were still in power.

Three grand houses in Loutolim that I have had the privilege of visiting were attacked repeatedly by the Rane clan in the nineteenth and early twentieth centuries: the Miranda house, the Figueiredo house and the Fernandes house, the third owned today by Lord Meghnad Desai, the well-known economist from London, and his wife, Kishwar, a writer. When Kishwar gave us a tour of her beautiful house during one of her lunch parties, she pointed out an embrasure in a wall behind the door facing the main entrance. These small openings hidden behind windows and doors in the big

---

4 Manohar Malgonkar, *Inside Goa* (Bardez: Architecture Autonomous, 2004, 1982), p. 111.

5 Ibid. p. 108.

mansions allowed their occupants to take cover while defending the house against bandits—with rifles if necessary. In the Miranda house, one could even draw in a staircase to hide safely on the upper floor.

The Ranes acted like a mafia clan. They never came unannounced, as Judith Borges, chatelaine of the Braganza house, told me. In true mafia style, they sent word stating what amount they wanted, on which day they would come to collect it and warning that they would attack if their demands were not met. Kustoba also attacked and burned police stations. Naturally, the Portuguese put a high price on his head. Mario and Habiba had a story to tell about him. One day, even as Constancio Miranda was on the hunt for Kustoba, whom he was later to kill, his wife was waiting by the Zuari river for a boat, when a canoe came by and offered to take her across. When she wanted to pay the stranger who had so kindly rowed her across, he declined, saying, 'Just tell your husband that the man who ferried you across is called Kustoba Rane.'[6] The story might be apocryphal, but then, as historian Pratima Kamat points out, the Rane myth is shrouded more in fable than in fact.[7]

Sadly, Mario Miranda died in his sleep, aged eighty-five, in December 2011. He and Habiba had lived in Bombay, but returned to live in their ancestral home in Goa for the last fifteen years of Mario's life. Habiba told me that in 1963, when Mario brought her to this house for the first time, she fell in love with Goa instantly. At that time the house had been abandoned for years, looted of

---

6 I first read about this story in Manohar Malgonkar, ibid. p. 112. The story was retold by Habiba in one of our conversations.
7 Ibid., p. 108.

its furniture and fittings, and had no electricity. Nevertheless, she insisted on spending the night in the house, sent the taxi driver to buy some provisions and they spent a memorably romantic evening cooking a meal there. That spirit of adventure and romance, the spell that the crumbling old family house cast on them, brought the Mirandas back to finally settle in Goa in 1996 and fill the Miranda house with life and laughter again.

Just a few weeks before Mario died, I had gone to see him and Habiba at home. Mario's sketches of Goan life are infused not just with his typical lightness and humour, but are also reflective and insightful in the way they capture human relationships, the spirit of a village and of family life.

The history of Goa's grand houses is closely intertwined with the rise and fall of the 451-year-long Portuguese rule in Goa. Today, these houses, with their unique and beautiful architecture, remind me of old ladies ageing gracefully—their joints might be aching, their purses stretched, but they retain their dignity and courtesy as they bravely keep up appearances.

7

Village Rituals

Village life, whether in Benaulim, Loutolim, Chandor or elsewhere, is shaped by and rooted in religious rituals and community feasts and celebrations that have smoothly made the transition from *Goa Portuguesa* to *Goa Indica*. Most of them are woven around events on the agricultural calendar, such as the rice harvest (the main harvest season being October) or the start of the fishing season. Both communities, Hindu and Catholic, follow the tradition of blessing the paddy fields. A few grains are then ceremonially carried to the church altar, or tied to the door in Hindu homes. When the fishing season starts after the monsoon, Catholic priests baptize new fishing boats and bless the fishermen before they venture out to sea. Throughout the year, there are feasts and festivals that knit the community together, and the church too plays an important role in this respect—for many Goan Catholics going to church is as much a part of their daily routine as brushing their teeth. Our priests in Germany would be overjoyed to receive just one-tenth of the usual turnout at any Sunday Mass in Goa.

I find the small ceremonies that are so meaningful to Benaulim villagers very moving. Take, for example, my neighbour John, who recently bought a second-hand bus—he earns his living by organizing trips for tourists. Lovingly and carefully, the whole family spent a day scrubbing and cleaning the bus, and the next morning prayers were said and the bus was blessed by Father

Benjamin Sacrafamalia in front of the Patricinio Chapel. 'You must not start anything without taking blessings first,' says John with his characteristic broad smile.

I am at times invited to the feasts and festivals held in our village. And of them, my absolute favourite is the beautiful annual procession of Our Lady, called *saibin*, which is held all over Goa, starting in September. It can last as long as three months, depending on the size of the village. The statue of Mary, adorning the church or chapel of a *vaddo* (village ward), is carried in procession to each house and placed on the family altar for one night. The following evening she is picked up by a group of neighbours and walked to another house, until all Catholic households have been blessed with her presence. 'We might fight here and there,' says one of my neighbours, 'and some neighbours might be troublesome, but when Our Lady comes to our house, or our neighbour's house, we are united and take each other's blessings.' I am not sure if this is a unique Goan tradition, but I have never seen or heard of 'sleepover parties' of church statues anywhere else in the Christian world.

My friend Marina tells me she thinks the tradition was introduced in the early years of Portuguese rule as a way of persuading Hindus to convert. It's certainly a plausible theory. The anthropologist in me sees this procession as a ritual worship of a Catholic mother goddess in what is very much a Hindu manner. Mother Mary is unquestionably the most important icon in Goan Christianity— my neighbour Tina points out that, in comparison, processions carrying the statue of Jesus through a village are rare, and even in these instances, Jesus never stays overnight.

In our ward, Pulwaddo Pequeno, which consists of approximately a hundred houses, there are three processions, each to a different part of the neighbourhood since the Patricinio Chapel has three altars with statues of Mary. The main altar is dedicated to Nossa Senhora do Patricinio. The oldest male of every house to which the statue is taken has the privilege of carrying her and neighbours join him to form a procession of around thirty to forty people, singing and holding candles. The priest of the ward is not a part of it. Each evening, the family hosting Mary for that night takes the responsibility of leading the liturgy. The altar is decorated with garlands, candles and twinkling electric lights. Firecrackers are set off, for Goans are crazy about crackers at every occasion, be it a birth, a marriage or a feast. The house is thoroughly cleaned before the procession enters and the statue is welcomed with a clay pot of incense. The entire family takes great care in choosing passages to be read from the Bible and the songs and prayers to be chanted. The prayers and singing last for about an hour, with all the generations of the family participating—some with bored faces, others fully engaged. Afterwards the family hosting Mary for the night provides snacks and drinks—in earlier times, a shot of feni and some gram; today, soda-pop, cake and paté. Although (as non-Christians) we were never offered the chance to host Mary in our house, I have been invited to the ceremony many times by my neighbours and friends. It is a beautiful bonding ceremony and my favourite village ritual because it evokes and cements a true sense of community. Being born into a Protestant family with several pastors on my mother's side (though my father was an atheist), I have always had an interest into religion and rituals. I left the Church when I was sixteen, studied Asian religions and, by an ironic twist of fate, have ended up living in an Indian village that is almost entirely Catholic. In Goa, I have met the most wonderful priests and nuns and seen a living church, with its humanity and its deeply meaningful rituals and community spirit, though it must be said that one also comes across stories of narrow-mindedness and bigotry. However, the priests are so idealized that it is not the priest himself, but the person bringing such stories to light who faces the anger of the parish. To mention just two such incidents: a doctor in north Goa, who had done many abortions, was told by a priest who had brought his maid to the clinic, 'Doctor, she must have done something called sex.' In another incident, very close to my own village, a priest was diagnosed with syphilis. When asked by the doctor to also bring his partner for treatment, the priest did not know 'whom of them to bring'.

Besides the traditional village rituals and feasts, there are some more recently adopted ones, such as those in honour of Our Lady of Health, Vailankanni, around whom a cult has grown in the past few decades. She can be found in many small shrines erected along the roadsides. And many fishing boats, taxis, buses and trucks are named after her, since Vailankanni is also regarded as the protector of vehicles and travellers. Half an hour south of my home, in a fishing village called Velim, people claim that she has appeared in visions and miracles have taken place in her name. Several of these events are said to have taken place in the 1980s, drawing thousands of curious spectators from all over Goa.[1]

One Vailankanni shrine stands by the road connecting my village Benaulim with Varca. Always decked with fresh garlands and candles, the shrine is located on a unique rock formation called the White Rocks, or Khoddpan, surrounded

---

1 Robert S. Newman, *Of Umbrellas, Goddesses and Dreams: Essays on Goan Culture and Society* (Mapusa: Other India Press, 2001), pp. 147–63.

by paddy fields. Whenever I pass by, which I do frequently, I see people with folded hands, their motorcycles and cars parked by the side of the road. The Khoddpan or White Rocks have an interesting history. It is said that in the old days temple dances were performed on the White Rocks in honour of the Goddess Dyaneshwari, also known as Goddess Santeri, a Goan goddess who was the focus of widespread worship before the Inquisition destroyed Hindu culture in Salcete. The knives used for slaughtering animals sacrificed to the mother goddess were sharpened on these rocks. One of the rocks is said to have an inscription (I could not find it, though) and people believe that whoever deciphers it will have the key to a great treasure that lies under the rock.[2]

Many Goan families host annual liturgies at shrines in their village, believing that this keeps alive the spirit of the shrine. The family of my neighbour Tina does this at the Khoddpan shrine annually and I eagerly accepted her invitation to join them once. Tina's father had started the family ritual several years ago, on Tina's birthday, after Tina's husband had recovered from a serious illness. After her father's death, she became responsible for keeping up the tradition and she hopes her son will continue it when she is no more. A crowd of around sixty people had gathered around the shrine, which was decorated with flowers. For almost an hour there were songs and prayers led by two elderly gentlemen. Afterwards, Tina's family distributed packages of home-cooked channa and rice, soft drinks and ice cream. Everyone sat on the sun-warmed rocks around the shrine, many of the guests dressed in their best

---

2 See 'Bannavli at a Glance'. *Bannauli*. Edited by Francisco Costa (Sanquelim: Konkani Seva Kendra, 1992), p. 19.

clothes, chatting and eating, before going back to their homes. I started to wonder why this Christian mother goddess, whose church is far away on the east coast of India, is so popular among Goans. Busloads of Goans, including many from Benaulim, go on a pilgrimage to Nagapattinam, a fishermen's village in Tamil Nadu, where Vailankanni's church stands. Three famous healing miracles are connected to Vailankanni, which led to the erection of her church in the seventeenth or eighteenth century in Tamil Nadu. Over time, the local cult became a national pilgrimage site. Her popularity today among Indians of all faiths (though mainly Christians) can be compared to the pilgrimage site of Lourdes in the south of France.

But the Vailankanni cult took root in Goa only in the 1960s after the 'Liberation'. Her popularity is thus a fairly new phenomenon. Her fame began to spread in the 1970s and many small shrines were built in her honour. So why do so many Goans believe in this miracle-working mother goddess and go (or aspire to go) to Nagapattinam?

In the times before the Portuguese conquest and conversion, the cult of the Hindu mother goddess was very strong in Goa, indicated by the many temples dedicated to her different forms. She was worshipped as Santeri (Goddess of the Anthill), Mauli or Shantadurga. This made it easy for converted Christians to adopt Mother Mary as a new form of the powerful mother goddess. This also might explain why Mother Mary in her many different forms seems to be so much more important than Jesus to most Goan Catholics. It is argued that, 'when large scale conversions are made from one religion to another, it is reasonable to assume that not everyone fully understands the new religion in its own terms. Rather, it is more likely that people will attempt to understand the new tradition in the terms of the old.'[3] Father Thomas Stephens, the first English priest who arrived in Goa in 1579 to study Konkani and Marathi, exemplified this understanding of a new tradition in terms of the old. He produced the first Marathi Bible in 1616, called *Christa Purana* (The Mythology of Christians), putting the essentials of Catholicism in a form familiar to local religious traditions. Today, a Konkani research institute in Alto Porvorim is named after him, since he produced the first Konkani dictionary as well.

Looking at the importance the mother goddess enjoyed in Goan Hindu culture before being wiped off the cultural landscape, it is probably no coincidence that Mother Mary is so popular among Goan Catholics and that processions and liturgies done in her name are so widespread. For many Goans it is she, rather than Jesus, who is the centrepiece of their faith.

The belief in faith healing and miracles is strong in our neighbouring village, Colva, where the main church, dedicated to Our Lady of Merces, houses a statue of Menino Jesus or Baby Jesus with a diamond ring. Local tradition has it that if the ring is kissed by devotees whose faith is strong and pure, then miracles can happen. Once a year, in October, the Colvenchem Fama—the celebrations of Infant Jesus—take place and Colva is jam-packed with people from all over Goa. They start trooping in at 4 a.m. that day to get a seat in the church for Mass, which starts at 5.30 a.m. The statue, kept in a bulletproof vault (to protect the miracle diamond ring), is taken in procession to a

---

3 Robert S. Newman, *Of Umbrellas, Goddesses and Dreams*, p. 202. He was also one of the first to point out the relationship between Hindu mother-goddess worship and Vailankanni.

nearby tree for blessing and brought back to the church dressed in new clothes, to be held out for public veneration and kissing. There is a popular story of how the statue came to Goa. The shipwrecked crew of a Portuguese fleet that survived a storm and swam ashore in Mozambique, found Menino Jesus—with his glistening diamond ring—sitting beautifully dressed on a rock, surrounded by birds. The statue was brought to Goa by the Jesuit Father Bento Ferreira and after he was posted to Colva in 1648, Menino Jesus was enthroned in a special altar, soon to become an object of veneration by the masses. It is believed that only the mummy of St Francis Xavier in the Basilica of Bom Jesus in Old Goa draws a larger crowd.

I have been to the Colvenchem Fama once and can never forget the sheer mass of people and the vendors blocking the roads, selling not only all kinds of household items, clothes and sweets, but also body parts made of wax to offer to Menino Jesus for healing. People stood patiently in queues for hours with crying infants and small children, awaiting their turn to quickly kiss the ring before being shoved out of the church by those behind them. Their faces shone with unquestioning and boundless faith.

It is village rituals and feasts like these, involving daily prayers as well as neighbourhood participation and community celebrations, that play a major role in shaping the Goan identity and character.

8

The Stoned Pig—Hippies and Neo-hippies

'Meet you in Goa for Christmas!' Forty years ago, that was a common refrain among travellers on the 'Hippie Trail'. Beginning in Europe and passing overland through Afghanistan and Nepal, the Hippie Trail culminated at Goa's Anjuna beach, where hippies congregated to spend the winter. Goa in December still remains a popular destination for Western travellers, but a lot has changed since those days when the hippies danced naked on the beach, stoned from morning to night.

When I first came to Goa, in 1987, there were many hippies among foreign travellers and the state still had virgin beaches. In 2012, twenty-five years later, I went back for a couple of days, curious to find out if Anjuna is still one of the few stops left on the old Hippie Trail, and whether any of the original hippies are still around. Do they still sit on the beach, watching their thousandth sunset? Do they interact at all with the tourists who now come on cheap charter flights and flood Goa's beaches? And what about the 'neo-hippies'? Do they hang out at Anjuna as well, or have they moved on to Palolem, Arambol and other, quieter beaches? How are they different from the old hippie tribe?

I was born in 1967, the legendary Californian 'summer of love' when 'flower children' formed a peace movement, believing they could change the world. They protested against the Vietnam War, believed in non-violent anarchy, showed awareness of environmental issues at a time when recycling and sustainable living were unknown to the mainstream, initiated a sexual revolution that spread from America to Europe, and questioned many social, political and moral norms, thus challenging and often scandalizing the establishment. Two years after the 'summer of love', the Woodstock festival took place, attracting half a million hippies, whose mantra was 'peace, love and unity'.

Though dismissed and laughed at by many, often with reason, those early hippies were not just a group of scattered 'freaks'. They may have been confused idealists, naive and self-absorbed in many ways, but they did constitute a distinctive counterculture, promoting a different philosophy of life that mocked the conservatives, questioned political certainties, family values and sexual attitudes and had a definite impact on the Western world.

The 'cultural revolution' of the hippies did not arise in a vacuum, but had its roots in the ideals of the earlier Beatniks who lived in California in the 1950s, rejected materialism, hitch-hiked everywhere, recited poetry, and explored drugs, alternative sexuality and Eastern religions in their quest for ultimate freedom and self-expression. The hippies (a word coined by Michael Fallon in a newspaper article in 1965 derived from being 'hip' or aware) followed in their footsteps.

To the horror of their parents, thousands of young people in the 1960s rejected the 'bourgeois repressions' they had been brought up with, and took off for the East in search of spirituality and self-knowledge. For them, India, a fabled country of mystery and magic, was the final destination—a land of cannabis-smoking godmen at whose feet they hoped to imbibe the eternal truths of life. Often they set off on their voyage with little or no money in their pockets. One such hippie was

Brigitte, a French girl from a well-to-do family who started her journey to India with 20 dollars sewn into her skirt.[1] Brigitte still comes back during the tourist season, where she can be found selling clothes she has designed herself, at Anjuna's famous flea market. Easily identified by their grubby clothes, hair, headbands and beads—the women without make-up or bra—travellers like her came overland via Ibiza, Morocco, Afghanistan and Nepal before reaching India, while their parents worriedly pored over such newspaper headlines as, 'Hippies begging like dogs in Afghanistan'.[2] In those days Afghanistan, which triggers very different associations today, welcomed the hippies with friendly curiosity. Mr Karimi, a Pashtun from Kabul who ran a camping place for hippies, recalls: 'At that time, we wondered why they had long hair and kept themselves so scruffy, but we did not laugh at them. Instead, we asked why they ran around like this. They wanted to be free and were tired of the fast, modern life of the West, they said. *That* we understood.'[3]

For many, such as Eight-Finger-Eddie, the Hippie Trail ended in Goa. Eight-Finger-Eddie came to Anjuna in the late 1960s and never left. Born Yertward Mazamanian to Armenian immigrants

---

1 Interviewed in German TV production *High sein, frei sein, überall dabei sein* by ARTE (http://www.arte.tv/de/high-sein-frei-sein-ueberall-dabei-sein-45/1592362.html).

2 *Times of London*, mentioned in Steve 'Madras' Devas, 'Our Only Story Is the Beach—The Life and Times of Amsterdam Dave', in *Goahead. Les Annees Folles: The Tribal Gathering* (2010), a photobook of the 1960s and 1970s printed for the reunion of hippies in 2010.

3 Quote (translated from German), in German TV production *Die Karawanne der Blumenkinder* by Maren Niemeyer, WDR and others, 2008.

in the US, 'he had nothing to return to', says an Anjuna local who had known him since he first arrived in the village. In summer, Eight-Finger-Eddie would go to Kathmandu to escape the Goan monsoon and 'hold court' at tea stalls, as one admirer fondly remembered on Facebook, most probably in the famous Freak Street off Kathmandu's Durbar Square. (Freak Street still exists but is now only a shadow of its former avatar as a hippie Mecca.) Eight-Finger-Eddie, a legend in his time, died recently, in October 2010, aged eighty-five. His ashes were scattered on Anjuna beach and in the Anjuna flea market.

Eight-Finger-Eddie was a magnet who attracted hippies to Anjuna from all over the world. Without travel guides, the hippies relied on each other's tips and experiences. The Pudding Shop in Istanbul, which still stands near the Hagia Sophia, or Mr Karimi's camping place in Kabul were places on the Hippie Trail where almost every hippie landed up at some point or the other. Stories of a beach in Goa where a tribe and their king smoked non-stop and lay naked in the sun, made Anjuna a much-sought-after destination. 'Meet you in Goa for Christmas . . .'

The young travellers also came to Baga, Vagator, Arambol in the north, and Colva in south Goa. The Vaghcolamb Tallem, a beautiful lagoon at Palye beach, next to Arambol beach, was a haven for hippies in the mid-1970s and, in contrast to Anjuna, remains a hub of the neo-hippie scene today. Many veteran hippies have moved to the more beautiful and quiet Vagator and Arambol beaches and only come to Anjuna to meet old friends. But in the hippie heyday, it was Eight-Finger-Eddie and the flea market he started that made Anjuna the fabled hippie paradise.

Tony, an Anjuna local, recalls the day Eight-Finger-Eddie arrived: 'He came from Baga, walking over the hill where we used to take our goats to graze. He stopped at our house and asked if he could live in that ruin nearby. We said "sure" and he moved in.'

While most hippies were between eighteen and twenty-five years of age when they reached the golden beaches of Goa, Eight-Finger-Eddie was already in his forties. He became mentor, godfather and friend not only to many young and lost travellers, but also to the villagers in Anjuna, as one local, who wants to remain anonymous, says. In those days there were no restaurants in Anjuna, so Eight-Finger-Eddie started a 'soup kitchen' for hungry and broke travellers who arrived with dreams of getting high and dancing through moonlit nights. The hippies gathered almost daily at Eight-Finger-Eddie's house and everyone was welcome. Later in life, his routine changed. 'He woke up at dawn to dance for 45 minutes every day, played patience all morning and then walked into the café for lunch at the stroke of noon without fail. He played racquet ball on the beach in the afternoon and was the first customer in the same restaurant each night. If his luck was in, someone would buy him dessert.'[4]

What made Eight-Finger-Eddie the unquestioned king of the hippie tribe? He never wanted to be a leader, it just happened, and no one ever challenged his position, recalls another local. 'Everybody followed Eddie,' says Tony. 'He was like a sadhu, easy-going and a very good talker.' Some young hippies tried to turn him into their guru, but Eight-Finger-Eddie was dismissive: 'I am not enlightened, I am just older than you. If the Buddha was out there on my doorstep, I wouldn't go out to meet him. What can the Buddha do for me? Meditation is a waste of time. There

---

4   '8-Finger Eddie RIP' (http://eddiewoods.nl/?p=2117).

is no path.'[5] Another of his axioms was, 'The best thing is to be completely disillusioned about everything.'[6] All he wanted in life was to have a good time, dancing and enjoying each day as it came. He always had people around to entertain and was known for his dirty jokes (at times, he even got paid for telling them). Unlike most other hippies, Eight-Finger-Eddie was not into drugs, which might explain why he lived till he was eighty-five.

Members of the old hippie tribe, like Eight-Finger-Eddie, didn't care what others thought about the wisdom they had found or the path of life they had chosen. For them, what mattered was that they did whatever they wanted to do in life. As Eight-Finger-Eddie once said, 'I am not a worldly success, but that does not mean anything to me.'[7]

'You cannot imagine the days we have seen,' remarked a villager who knew the hippies intimately and was also a good friend of Eight-Finger-Eddie. Like Tony, he was a teenager when the foreigners arrived in Anjuna. 'Village life was no fun, people here were alcoholics and miserable.' He and a few others often sneaked off to the beach and were soon roped into all kinds of activities. The hippies taught him freedom, he said. 'They brought me up. I cannot tell their stories, it could get them into a lot of trouble. I will die with a lot of secrets, baby! . . . And now this village is a graveyard again.' Tony recalls that only he and two other Anjuna youngsters became part of the hippie tribe, 'and of the three of us, Glenn went into brown sugar and died'.

---

5 Ibid.

6 Goa Hippy Tribe, Eight-Finger-Eddie interview (http://www.youtube.com/watch?v=RPZV7l40r5I).

7 Ibid.

One Western parent writes about the hippie culture, 'When we heard about the hippies . . . we laughed at them. We condemned them, our children, for seeking a different future. We hated them for their flowers, for their love, and for their unmistakable rejection of every hideous, mistaken compromise that we had made throughout our hollow, money-bitten, frightened, adult lives.'[8] Interestingly, the old hippies seem to be as defensive about their values as their parents' generation must have been about their own.

The Western 'left over hippies' were friendly but reserved when I approached them. They did not share much. Perhaps they are just tired of being constantly seen as a flock of colourful, crazy birds. The Anjuna flea market and the Saturday Night Market are places where one still runs into them. They drive by on their Royal Enfields and hang around in the bars and shacks of the northern beach belt. In Anjuna, you find them lunching at Joe Banana's, a restaurant that is something of an institution now, while O' Manuel O' is where they congregate for sunset drinks. They stick together and share memories of their lost paradise with each other.

The hippies of the 1970s had odd names. Eight-Finger-Eddie's name derived from the fact that he was born with only three fingers on his right hand. Others took names such as Curd-Tree, Woody Pumpernickel, Trumpet-Steve, Tarot-Ray, Amsterdam-Dave, Mushroom-Jack or Junkie-Robert. Shaking off their old lives, they arrived with these new monikers and often never revealed their original names or anything about their past. Many of them died young. Having shared the holy cannabis smoke and hanging out only with each other, the old hippies now introspect about how

---

8 June Jordan, Urban Dictionary (http://www.urbandictionary.com/define.php?term=hippie).

connected they really were. One of them recalls, 'Sometimes I think it's like we are all prisoners together. Okay, it was paradise and the drugs were good (unless you were flipped and fell in the well).' The same hippie asks, 'Who were all the guys that I did so much time with on Anjuna beach?'[9] On the surface, covering loneliness and unresolved issues with fun and frivolity, and dressing wounds with drugs—that is the other darker side of this hippie paradise. Nostalgic memories push aside ambivalences, lies and regrets. I wonder about the many secrets the dead and the living have locked up in their hearts. When one flips through the book *Goahead*, it is shocking to see that almost half the photos are marked RIP (rest in peace). The book consists almost entirely of snapshots of hippies, a 'souvenir' celebrating the reunion of the 'black sheep tribe' (as the hippies called themselves), which took place in north Goa in 2010. It is dedicated to those 'who got too close to the edge and never came back . . .'[10] Around 200 veteran hippies came together for this meeting. Some lead quite different lives today. Others still travel the world like nomads. At the reunion, the veteran hippies revisited their old haunts, one of them being Joe Banana's.

Anybody who spends time in Anjuna comes across Joe Banana. For the past forty years, his house has been a meeting point for hippies. Joe Banana is the hippie name of Diogo Almeida, a local from Anjuna. He was one of the few villagers who joined the hippies and smoked with them, as did his eldest son, Tony (whom you have encountered earlier in this chapter). Since he spoke good English, having worked in British Africa as a mechanic, he

9 Steve 'Madras' Devas, 'Our Only Story Is the Beach'.
10 *Goahead. Les Annees Folles: The Tribal Gathering.*

soon became a useful resource for the hippies, helping them in sundry ways and translating for them. Soon he started his own eatery on the veranda of his house. Says one local, who helped in the kitchen in the early years, 'In the beginning, you only got home-made peanut-butter sandwiches.' Apart from Eight-Finger-Eddie's 'soup kitchen' and two tea stalls called 'Buffalo Tea Stall' and 'Hindu Tea Stall', which were located on the north beach of Anjuna, Joe Banana's claims to be the first restaurant in Anjuna. Forty years later, Anjuna is so crowded with eating places, that it would take a year to try out all of them. Despite the profusion of restaurants, Joe Banana's—a plain, cemented space with asbestos sheets for a roof—still thrives. The lack of atmosphere is offset by the quality of its food and the many old associations. It's no wonder that the old hippies return to their temple. The restaurant is now run by Joe Banana's son, Tony, who lives in their ancestral house with his two brothers as a joint family. The three wives are the cooks. Unlike Tony, who was a part of the hippie scene in his teens (and gave up smoking only when he got married), his brothers and the three women seem untouched by the values of Western travellers. Then, as now, village life had a parallel reality. That in itself is a clear indicator of how most locals must have felt about the 'freaks' deep down in their hearts, even if 'good relations' were maintained on the surface. After all, most of the hippies were gentle people and it was thanks to them that the village economy was thriving. The villagers' real views on the hippies, which they share only with each other, will remain their secret. In terms of caste, the hippies were 'untouchables'. As I heard from different sources, local women would not marry them and made sure their children stayed far away as well. The hippies, inevitably, lived in their own ghettos.

In the 1970s, Joe Banana's was much more than an eating place. Passports and other valuables of the hippies were carefully wrapped in plastic and kept in the Almeida family safe. It also served as a 'lost and found' agency. Bags and other possessions, lost or forgotten by hippies high on drugs, were kept hanging on nails outside the house in the daytime and taken inside at night every day, till their owners turned up to claim them. Having been a central meeting point for hippies in the 1970s, it is no surprise that Joe Banana's served as the unofficial post office of Anjuna. The red wooden box, where letters for travellers were kept, still stands on the counter. It was enough to write the receiver's name—c/o Joe Banana, Anjuna, Goa—and the letter would reach its destination. 'Do letters still arrive?' I asked Tony. 'Sometimes.' Back in Benaulim I tried it out and posted an envelope in my name. Sure enough, when I returned to Anjuna a week later, my letter was there in the old letter box, in a bundle of other letters.

Apart from Joe Banana's, not too many traces of the lost hippie paradise are left in Anjuna. There are, of course, the many restaurants and shops run by former hippies, but most of these, such as the German Bakery or the organic restaurant Bean Me Up (two of my favourites), came much later. Today's hippies and travellers usually stay the winter months, many of them doing some small business in food, fashion or self-made jewellery to earn a modest income. They have their own boutiques and restaurants, and stalls at the Saturday Night Market and the Anjuna flea market.

The Anjuna flea market was started by Eight-Finger-Eddie and a bunch of hippies in 1974. In the beginning, around twenty or thirty hippies gathered every Wednesday to trade food and other commodities, such as cameras, clothes and spare parts for cars. Around the same time, *The Stoned Pig* appeared. The magazine, which lasted two years and published seven issues, carried ads for the Anjuna flea market. Without mobile phones or travel guidebooks, *The Stoned Pig* was the sole news disseminator in Goa, with tips, information and opinions of Western hippies.[11] The market grew and, over time, attracted not only hippies, but also Indian traders—in the beginning, mainly Lambani tribals from neighbouring Karnataka but later, traders from all over the country. In 1987, when I visited the flea market for the first time, people spread their goods on cotton sheets on the ground. There was little space to walk and one could chance upon small treasures to take home. It was a great experience. Today, it is much bigger, more commercial and offers mass-produced tourist tat. But that does not lessen its popularity among tourists, who come in busloads every Wednesday.

An innovative German started a second bazaar in Arpora in 1999 and called it the Saturday Night Market. Today it is the more popular of the two. Like everywhere else in the northern beach belt, one finds a lot of organic and wellness products at the Saturday Night Market. It is surprising how much the neo-hippie scene now engages with health food and wellness programmes. A closer look at blackboards in restaurants and shops reveals the great demand for colon-cleansing, yoga for kids, ashtanga and kundalini yoga, ayurvedic massage, African dance, martial arts, reiki, reflexology, healing detox programmes and so on. Catering to a group of mainly younger people searching for an 'alternative lifestyle', providing these services gives the neo-hippies, who do not need much to live on, a modest income.

---

11 The magazine was published in seven issues in 1975–6 by Tarot Ray; see also *Goahead. Les Annees Folles.*

One such example is the Russian neo-hippie scene in Arambol. My friend Deepa, who lives in Assagao, stumbled upon neo-hippies here and was impressed to see a group of Russians—complete with toddlers and older children—living in a commune just like the hippies had done forty years before them. For most of the neo-hippies, drugs seem to be passé but like their predecessors, they too are attracted to spiritual cults.

Many Western 'seekers' of the 1970s disappeared into ashrams, having found their spiritual guides. Some of these hippies-turned-sadhus are still around, like Swamy William from San Francisco, who insists that there is a connection between yoga and psychedelic drugs; or Rampuri Baba, also from San Francisco, who bought some land near Anjuna and wants to start his own ashram. Vinaya, an Indian from Bangalore who was once part of the hippie tribe and lives in a small 'commune' in Vagator (himself a kind of guru), is now cynical about hippies and Western sadhus. 'Earlier, the hippies were seekers; today they are really just tourists,' he says with a sigh.

A new generation in Goa has started to cash in on the hippie myth. Recently, in December 2011, a bar called Hippie's Ocean Café—with waiters in Hawaiian shirts—opened on Anjuna beach. It doubles as a trance and techno dance floor at night. I don't think any 'real' hippie ever sets foot there. It attracts tourists like me with its funny signboard in psychedelic neon colours, featuring a long-haired hippie and his Volkswagen van, a symbol of the 1970s when so many hippies arrived overland in this often beautifully painted vehicle.

Remembering Marcus Robbin's film, *Last Hippie Standing*, and curious to know what today's visitors make of hippies, I asked tourists at the Anjuna beach and flea market a simple question:

'What is a hippie?' Dozens of men and women from twelve different countries gave me their views and it was surprising how many came up with the same stereotypes. 'A hippie? I don't really know, but they are very cool.' 'Long hair, drugs, just chilled out from the world.' 'No idea. I think they are into music, like Second World War type of music, and like doping and bright colours.' 'Sex, drugs and rock 'n' roll.' 'Royal Enfield.' 'Flowers in the hair.' 'Drugs and smelly.' 'Doesn't like rules, likes partying.' 'Someone who is free in his mind.' The most original answer came from a six-year-old: 'Hippie is what you really like to do.' They're part of history now, the tribe that loved music; endlessly discussed which variety of hashish was the best, Mazar-i-Sharif or Manali; and rejected the values of their parents and of the 'materialistic Western world'.

Today, reggae is still played in the beach shacks, but the new generation no longer listens to the Rolling Stones, Pink Floyd, Janis Joplin or Jimmy Hendrix. Rave and techno are the sounds they prefer. The monotonous 'boom, boom, boom' makes you wonder how anyone can bear it without being high on psychedelic drugs, which most of the young Indians and foreigners are, as they dance through the night. Dozens of villagers offer sandwiches, cigarettes, sweets and other items at stalls which they set up in front of the rave-party hotspots along Anjuna beach. The parties rarely end before 3 a.m. The villagers must be inwardly fuming, since the techno music at the beach starts around breakfast and lasts till the wee hours of the next morning. But since most earn their money one way or the other from the techno–trance crowds, they keep quiet. You do not bite the hand that feeds you.

While drugs could be consumed freely in the late 1960s and 1970s, and could be smuggled to Europe and elsewhere easily, the Indian state tried to clamp down on drugs in the 1980s, passing, among other measures, the Narcotics and Psychotropic Substances Act of 1985. It did not really help. The drug mafia is too strong and the bribes they pay to the authorities too tempting. Drugs, therefore, are still rampant in Goa's clubs and beaches despite the many attempts by the few honest police officers to crack down on them. There is no drug that you cannot get in Anjuna today. As I was told, policemen who want a slice of this lucrative business have to pay at least a lakh of rupees as an 'entry fee'—an investment that will eventually yield rich returns in bribes. There are raids and arrests here and there, but honest policemen get transferred if they try to interfere, as happened recently with one cop who tried to 'clean up' Anjuna.[12]

When I first came to Goa in 1987, Anjuna was a quiet paradise, as it must have been in the 1970s. Above the counter at Xavier's restaurant hangs a painting depicting how the beach used to look. It's impossible to even imagine it today. In 1991, India opened up its economy and soon became a major global player. Over the past decade, globalization and economic growth have had their impact on Goa—construction, mining and other 'developmental' activities flourish without any effective control. The hippies might have been the first to put Goa on the world tourism map, but

12 See 'Police Whistle-Blower: SP Singh's Transfer an Influential Political Transfer', in GoaChronicle.com, 13 August 2013 (http://www.goachronicle.com/current-affairs/20141-police-whistle-blower-sp-singhs-transfer-an-influential-political-transfer%20/); Natalie Clarke, 'The Very Sinister Cover-Up behind Scarlett's Murder in Goa', in *Daily Mail*, 30 March 2008 (http://www.dailymail.co.uk/news/article-550611/The-sinister-cover-Scarletts-murder-Goa.html); Rupesh Samant, 'Police-Drug Mafia Nexus Exposed', in Goa News.com, 4 March 2010 (http://www.goanews.com/news_disp.php?newsid=1014).

their simple lifestyle did not harm the environment. The journalist Vivek Menezes observes about the neo-hippie phenomenon, '. . . tens of thousands of young people from India and abroad pour into places like Palolem and Arambol, and live happily in rustic (often dirty) huts and converted pig toilets, eat meals in a bewildering array of shacks, and party into the night on the beach. There are surely things to dislike about this model, but there are also significant positives. For one, the ecological harm caused is a tiny fraction of the corporate tourism sector. If you take away the temporary huts, shacks and tents on Palolem beach, magnificent coconut groves will still remain largely the way they have always been, because the footprint of tourism there has been minimally invasive. But look at Sinquerim or Varca, or any number of formerly precious, uniquely beautiful Goan locations that have been submerged under a tidal wave of grotesque concrete buildings. The dreadful mistakes are immediately evident, and we have to ensure they are not repeated.'[13] These 'dreadful mistakes' started in the mid-1980s, when charter flights started coming into Goa and unregulated construction destroyed the natural beauty of many coastal villages. Unless Goans wake up now, in another ten or twenty years there will be little left in the state to attract tourists. This is what happened in parts of Spain, for example, where overdevelopment drove away tourists, who moved on to other cheaper, more unspoilt places. What will happen, then, to the thousands of families on Goa's coastal belt that depend on tourism for their livelihood? There's little today to attract me to Baga, Calangute or Anjuna, except for some good

---

13 Vivek Menezes, 'Goa 2061: Threats, Challenges, Opportunities'. *Libertação 1961–2011*. Edited by Vivek Menezes, p. 150.

restaurants and boutiques. Anjuna beach is today more famous for the brutal murder of fifteen-year-old Scarlett Keeling, who was high on drugs and allegedly raped by seventeen local men in 2008, none of whom is behind bars. The old hippie paradise has metamorphosed into a raucous, crowded, commercial sprawl and the neo-hippies have moved on to quieter beaches to stage their cosmic dance. But the old tribe isn't quite forgotten yet. Walking towards south Anjuna beach, I find a poignant epitaph to two old-timers inscribed on a tile set into a crucifix. It says: 'Where Is 8 Finger?' and 'Amsterdam Dave Is Gone'. And surely this sign at the gate of an Anjuna house also dates to the hippie heyday: 'Beware of dogs, they smell, lick, taste, bite, chew and swallow. But most of all, be careful of the owner.'

Don't worry, be hippie . . .

9

Nustiyachi Koddi: Fish Curry and Rice

Vindaloo, xacuti, cafreal, fried and curried seafood—these are the dishes usually presented as 'local specialities' on the menus of restaurants and beach shacks patronized by tourists in Goa. But Goa's delicious and distinctive cuisine, one of the joys of living here, is in fact far more rich and varied, and a marvellous fusion of influences from different lands and traditions. To begin with, there are, broadly, two distinct traditions—Goan Catholic and Goan Hindu cuisine, the latter the preserve of the state's Saraswat Brahmins.

The Saraswat Brahmins are a small but influential community in Goa, making up around 3 to 5 per cent of the population (which is roughly 60 per cent Hindu, 30 per cent Catholic and 10 per cent Muslim). There are other Saraswat communities to be found in north and south India, but only the Saraswats of Goa and the west coast are known as 'Gaud Saraswats'. Saraswat cooking is heavily reliant on coconut, chilli and tamarind, together with vegetables like gourds and pumpkins, lentils and rice, accompanied by pickle and *papad*—all of this adding up to a balanced and healthy meal, especially since traditional family recipes are often based on ayurvedic medical principles. In addition, fish occupies a special place in Saraswat cuisine, since Saraswat Brahmins (like Bengali Brahmins) love fish and no meal is considered complete without it. Because fish is given such importance, going to the market to buy fish is a male thing, while the rest of the shopping is happily left to women. Goan men can get into a passionate conversation about fish the way French men do about wine. The fish that are favourites on the Goan table are mackerel (*bangda*), sardine (*tallê*), kingfish (*viswan*), bekti (*chanak*) and ladyfish (*muddashi*), while clams, prawns, crabs (preferably with lots of egg roe) and oysters come a close second. One of my many happy food memories in Goa is of the amazing river crabs I ate in a small dhaba run by a single woman, Esperanza, in the village of Rachol in south Goa. Only locals come to this modest place, which looks like a bar from the outside, but has much more to offer than just liquor. Her fried smoked mackerel and ladyfish are delectable, as are her prawn dishes—the smaller prawns and dried prawns are made into curries, while the big prawns and large brackish water 'white' prawns are served 'masala-fried'. Raj Salgaocar, a Saraswat Brahmin and a well-known industrialist of Goa, recalling his mother's cooking, says, 'Traditionally we add to the fish various seasonal fruits or vegetables grown locally, like raw mango, *bimbal*, hog berry (*ambado*), acrid lemon (*tefal*), drumstick (*mashing*), cocum (*sola*) and so on, which enhance the taste of the curry.'[1]

Some Saraswats now even eat chicken and mutton—unthinkable in earlier times—and only refrain from pork or beef which are favourites of the Catholic Goans. To make their food and culture more widely known, the Saraswat community has for the past twelve years organized an annual Saraswat food festival. Last year, it was held in February. Don't miss it if you happen to be in Goa at this time—you will taste the rich bounty of Goa's land

---

1 'A Saraswat Way of Life', in *Upper Crust* (http://www.uppercrustindia.
   com/oldsite/32crust/travels_20080303_24.html).

and sea in a sumptuous array of dishes where flavours, textures and nutritional qualities are finely judged and beautifully balanced. Mr Prabhudesai of Margao, president of the Mathagramasth Saraswat Samaj, says the food festivals also help reinforce among young Saraswat Brahmins confidence and pride in their rich culture.

However, most tourists, whether Indian or foreign, associate Goan food with Catholic cuisine, since the coastal belt is predominantly Catholic. The vindaloos, cafreals and xacutis dished up at beach shacks and coastal resorts are all typically Catholic dishes. Coconut—its oil, milk and grated flesh—features prominently in both Hindu and Catholic cuisine. So much so that more than 100 million coconuts are harvested annually in Goa, most of them consumed locally. Coconut oil, earlier discouraged for its high cholesterol content, is today hailed as one of the most beneficial of oils. The latest research claims that the ketones in coconut oil even prevent or slow down the progression of Alzheimer's disease. Another staple common to both communities is rice. The local variety favoured by Goans is reddish in colour and is husked and parboiled before being dried. It has a deliciously nutty taste. There is, however, a difference between how Hindus and Catholics cook their rice: Catholics boil it with salt, while Goan Hindus would not do this. In fact, an edict issued in 1736 by the Portuguese during the Inquisition, taking note of this difference and clearly targeting Hindus, expressly forbade Goans from cooking their rice without salt. *Kokum*, a sour red fruit that has medicinal properties and is valued as an antiseptic, is also common to both communities. It is used to flavour fish curries, but is also mixed with coconut milk and garlic, to be eaten at the end of a meal like a curry with some leftover rice, since kokum is known for its digestive benefits. A sherbet of the kokum fruit, mixing the syrup with ice-water or soda, is also popular and makes a very refreshing drink on a hot summer day.

Both Hindu and Catholic cuisine in Goa generally involves liberal amounts of spices—among them chilli, turmeric, pepper and ginger—and each family has its own combination, often a carefully guarded secret. When freshly ground, as they still are in village homes, the spices have a most tantalizing aroma, though many households now use an electric mixer. Convenient, of course, but not as tasty as those ground on a stone (we stick to grinding them by hand, though not all of them). When we bought our house, we found the old grinding stones in the garden at the rear where the kitchen used to be, and there they still lie, too heavy to be lifted. Our cat Jakob likes to curl up on them for a snooze. Modern supermarkets in Goa, such as Newtons, also stock prepared 'wet masalas', sealed in plastic. Visitors find these a convenient way to take home a bit of the taste and flavour of Goa. But almost every Goan I meet far from his home state reminisces nostalgically about the particular taste of their grandmother's *nustiyachi koddi* (fish curry and rice) or the aroma of a tall glass of feni (cashew nut liquor—and more about this later). One of the most apparent differences between Hindu and Catholic food is in the use of vinegar—it is taboo in Hindu cooking, but an essential ingredient in many Catholic dishes, such as vindaloo, balchão or sorpotel. Vinegar (as so many other food items and plants) was introduced by the Portuguese. It helped to preserve dishes at a time when refrigerators did not exist. Goan vinegar is special, since it is made from the sap of the coconut palm tree. The sap is mainly used to produce toddy (*sur*), a popular and cheap alcoholic beverage, since a coconut tree yields more than

400 litres of toddy per year. The sap is collected by the toddy tapper (*rendeir*) in an earthen container (*damonem*) and begins to ferment within a couple of hours. When it is fermented for a longer period of time, it becomes vinegar. The traditional process for making vinegar involved dipping a heated piece of roof tile into the coconut toddy—for what purpose, no one can tell me today. Toddy also serves as a yeast substitute, because yeast was unavailable earlier. It gives a distinct taste to bread as well as *sanna*, the latter being a steamed rice-cake, similar to *idlis*, made from rice flour and ground coconut. It is a delight for the taste buds to eat a sweetish sanna dipped into a spicy Goan prawn or meat curry.

There are many varieties of breads, consumed by Hindus and Catholics alike, but bread made with toddy is usually only eaten by Catholics. Bakers in Goa are always Catholic, since bakeries were introduced by the Portuguese. The artist Subodh Kerkar told me that the ancestral roots of these baker families are in the village of Majorda, a fifteen-minute drive from our house. My favourite bakery is Jila, located in a small village called Ambora (near Loutolim). Another historic place is the Confeitaria 31 de Janeiro in a back lane in Fontainhas (Panjim) and if you do take a stroll around the Mapusa Friday market, check out St Joseph Bakery.

The squeaking horn of the bread man as he carries a basket full of *pão* (Goan bread rolls) and cycles through the village lanes, wakes up all the households in our neighbourhood with its loud and persistent *poin-pum, poin-pum, poin-pum*. Whether eaten with butter and jam for breakfast or dipped into a hot lentil-and-vegetable curry, the Goans love their pão and often have it at lunch or dinner as well.

Before bread became a common breakfast item, people ate

canjee for breakfast (and still often do in the Goan hinterland). Canjee is a soupy, starchy rice-water, traditionally cooked in a container called *modki*. I find it makes for a healthy, sustaining start to the day.

Unlike Goan Saraswat and Hindu cuisine, which is said to be similar to Malvani (Konkan) and Mangalorean cuisine, the Portuguese influence on Catholic cuisine, which is strong on non-vegetarian dishes, is unmistakable. Apart from seafood, which is important for all Goans, it is mainly Catholics who eat mutton, chicken, beef and pork, the latter two forcibly introduced by the Portuguese in order to separate Catholic converts from their former Hindu communities. In Hindu culture, eating forbidden foods, such as beef, was one of the greatest taboos, and breaking this led to expulsion from one's caste. Aware that food was a powerful means to break family and community ties, the Portuguese used it as a tool to achieve this. During the Inquisition, for example, it was a punishable offence to reject pork as a Catholic, and it thus became impossible for the convert to share a meal with his family ever again. In old Portuguese mansions, such as the Braganza house in Chandor, one can still see three big tables in the impressive dining hall, reflecting the importance of food restrictions—one table was meant for Hindu guests, another for Muslims and the third for Christians, all served their separate foods. Today, most Goan Hindus and Catholics have no problem dining together at one table, sharing their food, as long as there is no pork or beef served to a Hindu.

While it might have been difficult for a new convert to eat pork 500 years ago, today pork is popular among all Catholics. There is no other community in India that is so wildly in love with its pork dishes and there is hardly a Catholic home in our village without its own pigs running around in the yard. I consider these pigs happy animals—they roam around freely—but when it comes to turning them into sausage and vindaloo, it breaks my heart to see how brutally their last moments are spent, carried upside down on a motorcycle between the legs of the person riding it, their legs and muzzle tied together on their trip to the butcher. One of our neighbours, a butcher, used to slaughter pigs at regular intervals, before he died of a heart attack. In the evenings he chased and locked the pigs in a shed, opposite our bedroom. I would hear them cry all night. Being intelligent animals, they must have sensed their fate. At five in the morning, I used to hear their dreadful screams as their throats were slit, and by nine they were hacked to pieces and sold at a stall at the crossing.

Dishes like *cabidela*, where fresh pig blood is stirred into the pork dish, are considered a delicacy. Sorpotel (only eaten on festive days, such as Christmas) is another famous pork dish, where pork meat, along with the liver, heart and kidneys, are cooked in a thick and very spicy sauce flavoured with feni. The flavour of sorpotel is said to improve with time and it tastes better each time it is reheated.[2] To the disappointment of some of our Goan Catholic hosts, I have never been able to bring myself to eat sorpotel or, for that matter, any pork dishes, except the famous spicy Goan pork sausage, *chouriço*. A modified version of the Portuguese sausage, chouriço is prepared from highly salted cubes of pork spiced with chilli and vinegar that are stuffed into the washed intestines of the slaughtered animal. These strings of sausages are then dried

---

2 Fatima de Silva Gracias, 'The Journey of Goan food', india-seminar.com (http://www.india-seminar.com/2004/543/543%20fatima%20de%20 silva%20gracias.htm).

in the sun and later gradually smoked on an open kitchen fire of the dry leaves, stems and husks of the coconut. Women from my village still come to collect these from my garden.

When, earlier, people used to stock up food for the monsoons, during which period fish was unavailable or expensive, these sausages, served with a spicy sauce, were especially popular. So were dried fish such as bangda, *kochudde, solaie*, strips of shark (*mori*), dried prawn (*suki sungttam*) and dried shrimp (*galmo*), which Goan homes used to start stocking up before the monsoons.

I have never got used to the taste of dried fish or prawn in a curry, although most Goans love it. But I love the dark red recheido sauce, which is used to marinate fresh fish and meats in Catholic cuisine. Whenever I order a fresh fish fillet at the beach, it has to be done recheido (also called masala-fry), cooked in a wonderful marinade of chillies, garlic, turmeric, palm vinegar, ginger, cloves, tamarind, onion and cinnamon. Vindaloo, perhaps the most famous Goan Catholic dish (and now next only to chicken tikka masala as a British favourite), also depends on a special marinade, this one made of vinegar or wine, and garlic (*vinho e alho* in Portuguese, hence its name). Balchão is a dish that originated in the Portuguese colony of Macao, where the marinade is made from shrimp, liquor, bay leaves, lemon and chillies. Xacuti, a spicy curry usually made with chicken (though it is also good as a vegetarian dish), has a sauce made with coconut milk, roasted and grated coconut, onion, green coriander and spices. It is popular among Western tourists since it is milder than vindaloo and yet has a distinct spicy flavour. There are not many vegetable dishes in Goan Catholic cuisine, so for a vegetarian, eating in Goa is only half the fun—they are much better off in Gujarat with its superb vegetarian cuisine.

Goa is today famous for its cashew nuts and feni, but not many people remember that cashew trees originally came from Brazil, introduced to Goa by the Portuguese to control erosion and to increase the forest cover. Today, 52,000 hectares (around 520 square kilometres) of land is under cashew cultivation. The Mughals called this strange nut 'badam-i-firangi' (the foreigner's almond). The cashew industry, which was properly developed only at the end of the nineteenth century, is now an important asset to Goa's economy, and the nut is exported to the rest of India and all over the world. As for feni, the potent cashew nut liquor, it is important to Goa's social life, infusing it with high spirits and cheer! You see makeshift feni stalls under thatched roofs all over the state, but my Goan friends tell me the best feni is made by Catholic priests in the village of Raia, where it is poured into clay pots and buried underground to mature until the fiery rawness has gone. So if you want to taste good feni, befriend a Goan priest ...

So much of the food eaten in Goa today was introduced by the Portuguese—chillies, potatoes, tomatoes, pumpkin, aubergines; the guava and jackfruit now growing in almost every garden, the pineapple, papaya (nicknamed 'tree melon' in Europe at that time) and the chikoo (called sapodilla in South America). The best mango varieties, such as Afonso, Costa, Malcurada, Fernandina, Xavier and Monserrate, were all grafted by Jesuits in Goa and exported to countries like Brazil. What would Goan food be like without these gifts from Portuguese colonialism? Even the milky, sugary tea and coffee dispensed from roadside stalls all over the state and consumed in every Goan home were introduced as recently as the nineteenth century, to be precise, after the Anglo-Portuguese treaty of 1878.[3]

Goan food also has African influences thanks to Goa's maritime links with Mozambique, the Portuguese colony from where slaves were procured for the empire. The famous and spicy cafreal, a favourite among Goans and tourists alike, where chicken is marinated in a sauce of chillies, garlic and ginger, and then dry-fried, got its name from 'kaffir', an Arab word referring to the African people (in Arabic, 'kaffir' just meant 'non-believer', it did not always have the racial connotations it has today). This dish is said to have been introduced to Goa by slaves from Mozambique.

Not all the new foods introduced by the Portuguese found ready acceptance among the Goans. The Hindus, for example, shunned potatoes and tomatoes which were regarded as 'impure'—they only found acceptance in the Hindu kitchen by the end of the nineteenth century. For this reason it is rare to find dishes with tomatoes when special Hindu festivals are celebrated, such as Ganesh Chaturthi, the most important Hindu festival in Goa.

Chillies, however, found instant acceptance among both Hindus and Catholics as a substitute for black pepper, which had become a highly priced export commodity, unaffordable for locals. Today, black pepper is the world's most traded spice. But there was a time when pepper was so rare and expensive, it was counted as one of the five luxuries in trade with the Roman

---

3 Fatima de Silva Gracias, 'Trail of the Aroma'. *Libertação 1961–2011.* Edited by Vivek Menezes, p. 104.

Empire (ivory, amber, silk and incense being the other four).[4] A kilogram of black pepper was as valuable as a kilogram of gold. In 1524, Indian traders were stoned to death on the streets of Goa when they tried to break the Portuguese monopoly of the pepper trade. The unbelievable riches that a few corrupt politicians and companies earn through mining today can perhaps be compared to the 'easy money' made with pepper and spices in the sixteenth century. Five hundred years later, the Germans still dismissively call the very rich 'Pfeffersäcke'—pepper-sacks!

I grow my own organic pepper and have also planted other spices for fun, such as cinnamon, nutmeg and vanilla. The pepper plant is a vine that climbs up coconut trees. It is not demanding, it just wants to be watered daily. Every February, after it has been harvested and dried, my friends around the globe get their fresh annual supply of black pepper, much better than anything you can buy abroad.

Goan cuisine is a reflection of Goa's history, showing the full diversity of this tiny, beautiful state's cultural fabric, a delectable fusion of influences from the Arabs, Konkans, Portuguese, Brazilians, Malabar, Malaysians, Africans and even the Chinese. What's distinct and home-grown is the Goans' deep enjoyment of food and drink, and their generous tradition of hospitality, according to which they never miss an opportunity to prepare a hearty feast, whether it's for a wedding, a saint's day or a local festival, and graciously invite friends, neighbours and strangers

---

4   Weighed out like gold, black pepper even served as currency to pay taxes, dowries, tributes and rent. When Rome was captured by Alaric the Goth in AD 410, he demanded 3000 pounds of black pepper as ransom. The Romans promptly complied (http://www.mccormick.com/Spices101/Enspicelopedia/Black%20Pepper.aspx).

to share it with them. A laden table and lavish hospitality are a matter of honour for Goans—and it is never more evident than at Christmas.

10

Moving towards Christmas

'Go easy on the food, drink and sex—remember it's Jesus's birthday, not yours!' wrote a friend from north Goa, veteran of many merry Christmas parties in Goa. Christmas in Goa's coastal belt is indeed a full-blooded celebration.

Preparations begin a good month in advance. Houses are whitewashed and thoroughly cleaned; cloth is bought and handed to the tailor to make the dresses that will be worn at the Christmas Eve Midnight Mass and on New Year's Day, when the church is brimming with people—a prime occasion for women to show off their fashion sense and elegance. All through December, I see our village tailor going at it, bent over his sewing machine from early in the morning till late at night. The men, meanwhile, begin work on the community cribs—more about these later. Around a couple of weeks before Christmas, my neighbour's children come and ask to cut bamboo from our garden to make paper Christmas stars and also build a family crib. Electrical wiring for the many stars and colourful lights that decorate the houses and the village is bought, the church is cleaned by groups of village women and the children prepare for their roles at the Midnight Mass, whether it is singing or playing angels on stage. And most importantly, in all households, the women get busy making special Christmas treats.

Goa has a long tradition of home-made Christmas sweets, with families gifting plates of *kokad* (a crunchy coconut-and-semolina sweet cooked on a slow fire), Bebinca (made of egg yolk, flour, coconut and sugar), *dodol* (a fudge made of jaggery, rice flour, coconut and cashew nuts), *doce* (a confection of chickpeas and coconut) and *kormola* (tiny deep-fried sweets made from flour, ghee, eggs, sugar and coconut milk) to neighbours, friends and relatives. Every year, on Christmas Day, we too receive these delicious platters overflowing with kokad, dodol and doce.

In earlier times, when villagers took turns to help each other farm their land, cooking and baking in the festive season also used to be a community activity. The women of the village would work in each other's kitchens to prepare *kunsvar*, the traditional festive sweets sent to neighbours and friends, most of which take a lot of time and labour. Now most Catholic households prepare their own sweets, supplementing them with confectionery bought from local bakeries. Some of the best bakeries are old family concerns in places like Majorda, Mapusa and Panjim.

Like the rest of Goan cuisine, Goan sweets too are a fusion of different influences and eras. Writes Fatima de Silva Gracias, 'It has often been pointed out that the nuns of the Convento da Santa Monica in the old city of Goa were responsible for . . . introducing Portuguese recipes, and for creating the Indo-Portuguese recipes, particularly sweets like *dedos da damma* (a kind of marzipan), *petas de freiras, pasteis de natas, pasteis de Santa Clara*. These sweets are still served as dessert in some Goan-Christian homes on festive occasions.'[1] Even Bebinca, the delicious multilayered dessert for which Goa is famous, is said to have its origin in Indonesia, Malaysia and the Philippines. To bake the traditional

1 Fatima de Silva Gracias, 'Trail of the Aroma'. *Libertação 1961–2011*. Edited by Vivek Menezes, p. 104.

seven layers of the Bebinca (the number of layers varies, people say in the old days that number used to be forty) takes around eight hours and a lot of skill (I don't have either the patience or the skill to attempt it myself). But I've noticed the children in our village enthusiastically and uncomplainingly help their mothers make the Christmas goodies as well as the decorations.

Nowadays the Christmas trees that are set up inside the homes are made of plastic and decorated with glitter, stars and cotton flakes. But earlier, every Christian home had a Japanese tree with needle-like leaves (it grows well in the tropics) planted in their front yard, which used to be decorated each Christmas. One can still find these trees in the front yards of old houses. The sound of Christmas carols is all-pervasive—blaring all day from someone's radio in the neighbourhood, or sung by children moving in groups around the village and the beach, hoping for a few rupees or sweets, which they share at the end of the evening.

Hindus too join in the Christmas celebrations, but nowhere is it as alive as in the coastal belt populated in the majority by Catholics. I avoid driving into town the week before Christmas— too many people, too much noise and too much pushing around; the markets overflowing with food and Christmas decorations, and people shopping for last-minute gifts.

The frenzy before Christmas Day culminates in the Midnight Mass, usually conducted in Konkani. This most important Mass ends around two in the morning, after which firecrackers are set off, and the community cribs that are scattered along the sides of major village roads are unveiled.

The cribs in Goa, built by the men of the village, are a magnificent sight. The care with which they are created and the detailing that goes into them are mind-boggling. Some are as big as a stage set and one can even walk right into a few. I often wonder why the same Goan men who lavish hours of such painstaking effort on these cribs don't put even a fraction of the same effort, ambition and enthusiasm into their professional work. Men of all ages are involved in this effort, though most of them are in their twenties and thirties. They start a month in advance, keeping the crib covered with big plastic sheets, so people cannot see what is being created. I often stop to chat with them and they tell me that they love to spend their time this way, working with friends, ending an evening's hard work on the crib with a drink at the local tavern and keeping out of the hair of the women at home who are busy making the Christmas sweets. Once the cribs are open for public viewing, it is interesting to observe these young, 'cool' men on their motorcycles, hanging around after dark near the crib they have helped to build, while people come to watch, comment and take photographs. They bask happily in the compliments they get and wonder whose crib will win the competition. For there is indeed an official competition of community cribs, with a bona fide team of judges going around assessing the creations. Though only a few community cribs are entered in this competition, the men are inspired to come up with new ideas and each year they get more and more inventive. Thus one sees cribs with the Sphinx and Egyptian pyramids; with electricity-run waterfalls; carefully constructed bridges over ponds and rivers, sometimes with live fish in them (in one of the bigger cribs they even had ducks); sheds for Mary, Joseph and the newborn baby Jesus with angels flying above; beautiful palaces for the three kings; or whole villages surrounded by miniature rice fields, gardens and hills; handcrafted crocodiles, sheep and other animals; a showerhead turned upside down to function as a fountain, and painted bottles as battlements of a castle tower. Clearly the creativity of the artists knows no bounds. Creating a crib for the family home is an old and widespread tradition in the Christian world. However, the tradition of creating huge community cribs within the village is not, as one might have thought, an old Goan tradition, but a fairly recent phenomenon. In earlier times, there was, perhaps, one big community crib on the premises of the village church. Today, especially in Benaulim, one finds a number of beautiful cribs all along the roads. In my village, I had counted over a dozen during Christmas a couple of years ago. One reason for this new trend is the growing amount of money available to the aam admi, which allows the villagers to spend on building materials for the cribs. Moreover, local MLAs give money to groups of young men for crib-building, basically as part of their effort to garner votes. Over the past few years, I have seen an interesting new development—cribs are being used to take community issues and environmental concerns across to people. It started after the 26/11 terrorist attacks in Bombay in 2008, with peace messages and images on the cribs of the Taj Hotel under siege, and went on to community issues such as illegal mining, corruption and the absence of an effective garbage-collection system.

Every year I drive around Benaulim and the neighbouring villages to have a look at the different cribs, usually with friends and visitors in tow. This ritual of crib-visiting almost has the character of a pilgrimage, with many Goan families also making the rounds, and halted cars and motorcycles holding up traffic and blocking the roads. In 2011, on one of these night trips, we bumped into a Christmas carnival procession, complete with a brass band and floats carrying all kinds of oversized animals, an aeroplane and stars. In true Goan style, the villagers were following, many dancing to the music blaring from loudspeakers. It was a delightful sight, capturing the easy-going, joyous spirit of Christmas in Goa's villages.

Christmas celebrations on the beach, however, are quite different. The period between Christmas and New Year is the most expensive time in Goa—prices everywhere suddenly shoot up and beach shacks are crowded till late into the night. Flights to Goa are unaffordable and booked out long in advance, hotel room tariffs double and taxi rates go bananas. At the beach, where almost all tourists celebrate Christmas, bands play music night after night in different shacks, firecrackers are burst and, when the night gets chilly, the revellers sit around bonfires. There is plenty of food and drink and dancing till the wee hours, and for those looking for it, rave parties, drugs and lots of sex. Prominent among the tourists taking part in Christmas festivities on the beach are middle- and upper-class youngsters from Delhi, Bombay and other Indian cities. For them, Goa is a 'mythical paradise' of unlimited wine, women and song, and nowhere else in India do these young people feel so liberated from social inhibitions, middle-class mores and the disapproving gaze of their elders.

Their parents too congregate in Goa in winter. At times, going to a party in north Goa during the Christmas–New Year season is like being at a high-society event in Delhi—friends who are too busy to meet each other in Delhi catch up here (and then often carry on to the Jaipur Literature Festival which has become as much a social event as the New Year in Goa). Many of these people have invested in property in Goa—a villa or spacious flat, usually in 'happening' north Goa rather than sleepy south Goa, which remains empty the rest of the year. These winter visitors have their favourite restaurants and watering holes. In Candolim, for example, Pete's Shack is where Osho therapists have been meeting for the past twenty years; while the Delhi elite, dressed in stylish, carefully casual resort wear, can often be found in Morjim, at 'chic' hangouts like the beach restaurant La Plage.

Since we have so many friends (and friends of friends) pouring in over Christmas and New Year, we sometimes have a long table set up near the water at our favourite beach shack, where we order seafood platters in advance. Many of our most memorable Christmas dinners have taken place there, on the sand and under the stars.

For local people too, the festivities continue well after Christmas Day. There are afternoon and evening activities for children in every ward and church in the villages, and games in which people of all ages participate—I once saw a group of giggling old ladies competing in a 'candle-run'. On 31 December, the roads are inevitably blocked with dozens of young boys asking for a 'road tax' because it is the day of the 'Old Man', the Santo Munis, a Christian version of Ravana. In high spirits, the village youth stand all afternoon next to a life-size puppet they have made of the 'Old Man' representing evil, that will be burnt at midnight. The last event in this festive time is the Feast of Epiphany, celebrated in a special way for the past 400 years in Cansaulim, a village not too far from Benaulim. There is a beautiful little church on a hill overlooking the valley on one side and the village with its rice fields on the other. The church, constructed in 1599, is deserted—villagers tell me not to go there on my own, claiming a murder took place up there many years back. It is indeed a secluded but romantic place, with its arching trees and an amazing view. Only young lovers in search of some privacy can be found in the shade of the church walls. On 6 January, the day of Epiphany, however, the church and the hillock transform into a stage for its famous ceremonial act of the three kings. It attracts hundreds of spectators from all over Goa and has been celebrated since the seventeenth century, when the Portuguese granted Cansaulim, Arrossim and Cuelim the privilege of choosing a boy from each village representing the three kings, to thank the *gaunkars* (landowners) for supporting the Christianization of these villages. It is this festive procession, the day of Epiphany, that signals the end of the Christmas–New Year holidays. Then, the cribs are taken down and Goa, which had come to a semi-standstill, except for people working in tourism-related jobs, returns reluctantly to its routine and daily life.

11

Sacred Groves in Secret Forests

I first heard about the sacred groves in the hilly forests of Goa in 2007. These are areas whose inhabitants (tribal communities as well as Hindus) worship nature, spirits and local deities. In a state best known for the sand and surf of its coastal resorts, I was eager to explore these pristine habitats in Goa's hinterland. I have been attracted to such places since childhood, when my father used to take us sailing around the coasts of Scandinavia. When we anchored in a lonely bay, my siblings and I would set off to explore the nearby rocky islands, with their abandoned huts amidst thick coniferous forests. We would return to the boat thrilled with our booty of shells, weathered bones, pine cones and interestingly shaped stones.

Goa's sacred groves—called *devrais* (trees of the gods)—are 'believed to be under the control of deities or holy spirits and are thus revered and respected'.[1] Villagers have venerated these natural habitats for generations. Some of them contain old stones— scattered around a tree or sheltered in a temple-like structure—that

---

1 The sacred groves in Goa are known in different places by different names. In Sattari, they are called *devrais*, in Ponda *devgal*, in Sanguem *pann*, in Canacona *devaran* or *devadano*. See Rajendra Kerkar, 'Sacred Groves: Indigenous Institutions of Biodiversity Conservation'. *Multiple Dimensions of Global Environmental Change*. Edited by Sangita Sonak (New Delhi: TERI Press, 2006), p. 197.

are regarded as village deities. Others are connected to a village temple outside the sacred grove, as for example in Keri, a village in Sattari, close to Goa's largest sacred grove, the Ajobachi Rai, where prayers and animal-blood sacrifices are offered every Wednesday and Sunday in the temple of Sateri Kelbai. These are spaces— some of them small, others sprawled over several hectares—with majestic trees and springs and streams, rich in biodiversity, where locals believe the spirit or *devchar* of the deity lives.

The belief that spirits reside in trees, stones, paddy fields and lakes is still widespread, says the zoologist Manoj R. Borkar. They are appeased with offerings of all kinds, including chicken, toddy, bread and even leather shoes.[2] Such beliefs ensured the preservation and protection of large areas of forests in Goa in the old days. But now, because of the greed of miners and developers, and the consequent large-scale sale of land, Goa's remaining sacred groves are under threat.

Thanks to the environmentalist Rajendra Kerkar's tireless work, however, interest in and knowledge of these sacred groves and their cultural and ecological importance has been revived.[3] Since 2012, sacred groves in Goa are being explored in a more systematic way and documented in an All India Sacred Groves Project, where, among other things, their eco-dynamics, socio-biology and other aspects, such as water storage, are being studied.[4]

---

2 Manoj R. Borkar, 'Sacred Yet Scientific: Eco-Theological Basis of Biodiversity Conservation in Goa'. *Multiple Dimensions of Global Environmental Change*, pp. 184–5.

3 Most information on Goa's sacred groves is based on Rajendra Kerkar's newspaper articles, as well as a personal conversation with him in Keri, strolling around some of Keri's sacred groves.

4 Conversation with Manoj R. Borkar, 12 September 2012.

It was Rajendra who first wrote about the sacred groves in the village of Nanoda, named after the 'naked woman tree' (nano), guarded by the spirit Nirankar. What an enchanting idea to see a tree as a naked woman—a flight of imagination no doubt inspired by the smooth, glossy bark of the nano tree (*Lagerstroemia microcarpa*), which is similar to the eucalyptus. Another variation in the cult of tree worship is the abode of a female spirit known as Bhutachye Zhad. It is venerated by offering a small cane cradle filled with flowers, bangles, vermilion powder and other cosmetics in a village called Naingini, near Ponda.[5] Manoj Borkar told me it is the only tree where such offerings are made, since the basket-weaving community believes that if the female spirit is not appeased in this way, she has the power to harm newborn babies.[6]

The villages in the vicinity worship the spirit Nirankar in two different sacred groves. One of them is located in Nanoda village itself. The other, smaller one, located between Nanoda and Maloli, is believed to have existed for the last 250 years and is a site of great ecological significance. In the past, the residents of Maloli, Ustem and Nanoda got together at certain times of the year to worship Nirankar, who, as the protector of these villages, needed to be propitiated with a sacrifice to ward off evil and allow them to prosper.[7] Though the groves and the deity are still venerated, many of the rituals performed there are dying out now—victims of modern notions of rationality. Curious to find out more about the groves, I set off with some friends, driving through the forest

---

5 Manoj R. Borkar, 'Sacred Yet Scientific: Eco-Theological Basis of Biodiversity Conservation in Goa', p. 186.

6 Conversation with Manoj Borkar, 12 September 2012.

7 See Rajendra Kerkar, 'Sacred Groves: Indigenous Institutions of Biodiversity Conservation', p. 199.

with just two village names, Nanoda and Maloli, as my compass. We drove the whole day, going round in circles around Nanoda and Maloli, asking villagers for directions. We finally found the smaller of the two groves just next to a temple on the road. Ugly cement steps led down to a clear stream of water. I was disappointed: this sacred grove was a tiny space, just a clump of trees and bushes on marshy ground, with a single massive tree and strange aerial roots shaped like inverted Us. Having seen photographs of the site earlier, I had imagined the grove to be larger, cleaner and more thickly wooded. It was, however, easily recognizable from the photographs because of these uniquely shaped roots. I had read about it as a 'myristica swamp forest', an abode of rare medical plants, so I was dismayed to see it littered with garbage. Close to the grove was an old shuttered house with a fire burning inside. I tried to peep through one of the windows but could not see much—it looked like an illegal liquor brewery.

I experienced the magic and mystery of Goa's sacred groves only some months later, when I drove to Keri, a small village in the foothills of the Western Ghats, to meet Rajendra. Rajendra and his wife work as teachers and devote their free time to the preservation of Goa's environment. They are not the kind of activists 'who preach water but drink wine'. To give a small but telling example, when Rajendra once wrote to me, his note was scribbled on recycled paper and a used envelope turned inside out.

As we stood looking on to the vast grove called Ajobachi Rai on the outskirts of Keri, Rajendra held my attention with his stories. He talked about the beliefs connected to this place and how the villagers, irrespective of their caste and religion, guard it. Ajoba is the holy spirit that resides in this forest and people believe that those despoiling this place will face misfortune. Keri and its surroundings have the largest number of sacred groves[8]—ten in all, though only a few are well protected. He showed me two small ones, of which one was hidden amidst banana plants. It was a collection of deity stones arranged around a tree called 'beboll' by the locals that is known to be very poisonous—just standing under it leads to swellings and itching. Rajendra spoke of around 200 such sites that he had visited in Goa, most of them in the Western Ghats area of Sanguem, Canacona and Sattari taluka that have heavy forest cover and thus a concentration of *devrais*. A more conservative estimate of sacred groves in Goa is 100–150.[9] Some rare species of plants have been found in these sacred groves and since hunting is taboo, birds, reptiles and mammals, among them pangolins and Malabar giant squirrels, thrive in these undisturbed habitats.

Rajendra, however, has no illusions about the future of these groves: some of them are in imminent danger of being reduced in size and vegetation. Indeed, some, such as a once-famous sacred grove near the highway towards Mapusa, have already been completely destroyed.

Though sacred groves are found all over India[10] and indeed

---

8 Keri's sacred groves are named Ajobachi Rai (the biggest and most important), Baldyachi Rai, Comachi Rai, Birmanyachi Rai, Panvelichi Rai, Hornyachi Rai, Oralachi Rai, Pishyachi Rai, Abadurgyachi Rai and Maulichi Rai, situated between the Vagheri and Morlegad hills of Sahyadri.

9 Conversation with Manoj Borkar, 12 September 2012.

10 About 13,720 sacred groves have been counted so far from nineteen states in India (Bhandary and Chandrashekar, 2003, cited by Rajendra Kerkar, 'Sacred Groves: Indigenous Institutions of Biodiversity Conservation', pp. 196, 203).

in many cultures all over the world, to me there seems to be something special about the ones in Goa, perhaps because they allow one to enter a vanished past. The Portuguese Inquisition had destroyed much of Goa's vibrant religious culture and history in the (mistaken) belief that 'they could eliminate Hinduism by destroying the temples, implementing draconian conversion policies, and systematically discriminating against Hindus'.[11] But during the period of the Inquisition, much of Goa's hinterland had not yet become part of Portuguese territory. Thus many Hindu and tribal folk traditions, rituals and ceremonies in these areas survived intact. It is only now that these, including the many folk dances that had been alive and vibrant in the hinterland for centuries, are being threatened. Most Goans mention Dekhni or perhaps Mando, when you ask them about Goan folk dances, but, in fact, there are as many as fifty-five forms of folk dance, such as Morulo, Horbala or Zemaado, that are little known outside the hinterland. And some of them are connected to the sacred groves.[12] The film director Nandini Sousa and her production manager Rohit Phalgaonkar trekked through these areas to document these hidden traditions and perceived the folk dances they saw as an expression of 'worshipping nature through dance'.[13] Most of these dances are held on specific occasions at a

---

11 See P. Axelrod/M.A. Fuerch, 'Flight of the Deities: Hindu Resistance in Portuguese Goa'. *Modern Asian Studies* (Cambridge: Cambridge University Press, May 1996) Vol. 30(2), p. 391.

12 'Reviving Goa's Folk Dance Legacy', in *Navhind Times*, 18 July 2012 (http://www.navhindtimes.in/iexplore/reviving-goa-s-folk-dance-legacy).

13 The team has documented fourteen dances—the Morulo, Gawda Zagor, Ghoddemodnni, Dhalo by Velips of Canacona, Kallo, Fugdi from

sacred place called *maand*. Even Christianized tribals light a lamp before starting the dance, showing 'that they have not forgotten their roots'.[14]

One tribal community with a distinct culture is that of the Kunbis, called Curumbis by the Portuguese. The Kunbis are a hard-working, landless community of cultivators, mainly engaged in growing paddy in Salcete, the taluka I live in. The Kunbis, along with the Gowdas (another tribal community), are regarded by some historians as the earliest settlers of Goa, having lived here much before the arrival of the Brahmins.[15] They are known for their traditional medicine and believe that sickness is caused by evil spirits. It is said that they shy away from modern medicine because touching glass is taboo for them, and so, pills and tonics in glass bottles (as also alcohol or even tea in a glass) are not permitted.[16] The Gowdas, too, have deep knowledge about herbal medicine and it is believed that one of their formulas, handed down for generations, is the best treatment for hepatitis.[17]

Those Kunbis who have not been Christianized have their own deities. Apart from their *gram devata* (village deity), they also worship snakes, the tulsi plant (basil) and the wrathful Betal (also called Vetal), whose statues can be found in the forests. The fashion designer Wendell Rodricks has revived the vibrantly

---

Pernem, Tonymel, Goff, Mando, Talgadi, Khell Tiatr, Zemaado, Horbala (dance of Dhangar community) and Bhonvaddo. 'Reviving Goa's Folk Dance Legacy'.

14 Ibid.

15 S.R. Phal, *Society in Goa* (New Delhi: B.R. Publishing Corporation, 1982) pp. 37–8.

16 Ibid., p. 38.

17 Conversation with Manoj R. Borkar, 12 September 2012.

beautiful Kunbi sari, introducing it to the fashion world in 2010. During his research into Kunbi culture, he stumbled upon a nine-foot-tall Betal statue, believed to be from the ninth century, in the forest in Loliem, near the Aryadurga Mandir in Kazalker Vaddo. Being a guardian deity, Betal—a god with a hyper-masculine body and an oversized penis—is meant to evoke fear with his huge eyeballs and tusks. He is offered goats by the tribals, as well as alcohol, chapattis, rice and kane, a yellow flower—a ritual performed every Wednesday and Sunday by a man from the Devli tribal community.[18]

There are other tribal groups in Goa connected to the sacred groves, among them the Velips, who venerate dogs. The Velips settled in difficult hilly terrain, where dogs protected their crops against pests and intruders. They are hunters and worship a warrior-god called Paik, mounted on a horse with a sword in his hand.

Dhangars, a more docile community, worship stones smeared with vermilion and turmeric in their sacred groves, and make offerings of dates and coconuts.[19] Leading their lives in harmony with their surroundings, the Dhangars are known for their ecologically sound practices. The Gowdas, who comprise an agrarian community like the Kunbis, are renowned for their expertise in managing the network of dykes (*khazans*), a unique agricultural system in the coastal wetlands, which is also used for aquaculture and salt panning. Khazans are believed to have been

---

18 See Wendell Rodricks, *Moda Goa* (Noida: HarperCollins, 2012), pp. 15–19.

19 Manoj R. Borkar, 'Sacred Yet Scientific: Eco-Theological Basis of Biodiversity Conservation in Goa', p. 184.

created in the mangrove forests as early as in the pre-Christian era.[20]

The culture and traditions of Goa's tribal communities that, together with Hindu village folk, protect the sacred groves, are far removed from life in the bustling, often tacky, beach belt. I do not mean to idealize or romanticize Goa's tribal communities: the villagers live hard lives and are trapped in poverty. Often, driven by our pursuit of a 'spiritual anchor' to escape our stressful modern lifestyles and our own disconnect from nature, we project on to these communities an imagined life. Tribal and village life is far from being as idyllic as we are wont to believe. Most tribals today have not chosen their way of life—they follow the traditions of their forefathers because they have no choice and no way of experiencing other lifestyles. However, if we would listen more carefully to what they have to say and if they would be more sincerely respected for their invaluable knowledge of medicinal plants, food harvesting, water conservation and the whole cycle of nature, modern society could benefit a great deal from the practices that these marginalized people have kept alive over the centuries.

The villagers, whether tribal or Hindu, manage the sacred groves through 'social fencing'.[21] The customs and rituals, superstitions and fears connected to the groves and their spirits, ensure care and respect for their flora and fauna and enable the protection of their biodiversity. As Rajendra describes it, there are

---

20 However, the first documentation of khazans comes from a copper plate dating back to the sixth century AD, where a king donates khazan lands.
21 Pratima P. Kamat, *Goa, Its Tryst with Trade* (Panaji: Goa Chamber of Commerce and Industry, 2009), p. 25.

regulations regarding the felling of trees, grazing cattle, collection of leaf litter, wood and plants (except for medicinal use).[22] No one would dare to enter a sacred grove before praying to the gods and spirits, apologizing for the disturbance or asking permission to dig out a root that is needed for medicinal purposes.

Morpila, a beautiful, sleepy village in the taluka of Sanguem, is inhabited by the Velips. Driving past cashew plantations, I arrived there on a morning that happened to be the last day of a religious festival. I don't know if they had worshipped their forest spirit, Paik, or some other village deities that day, since the elders seemed reluctant to allow us 'strangers' to go with them to the temple inside their sacred grove, which they call *pann*, dotted with small clay statues of Paik astride his horse. Two young Velips from Morpila volunteered to accompany us when we asked to see the stream called Paikacho Vhal (stream of the forest spirit, Paik), which has been guarded by the Velips for generations. It was a memorably beautiful walk, but to reach the spot where the cascading Paikacho Vhal actually emerges from the forest, one would have had to crawl on all fours through thick bushes and vegetation. So we walked to a more accessible place where the villagers had constructed pipes to channel the crystal-clear water—the only water resource in this area—to the village.

Rajendra has committed himself to protecting not only the sacred groves but also the rituals and traditions of the people who live around them. For the past twenty years, he has travelled through villages in the hinterland, initiating public hearings that encourage villagers to take pride in their cultural heritage, to protest

22 Rajendra Kerkar, 'Sacred Groves: Indigenous Institutions of Biodiversity Conservation', p. 197.

and act against mining which is scarring this pristine landscape and to safeguard their deities that are scattered in the forests. Many of these, carved in stone,[23] lie around seemingly forgotten. They are visited and prayed to only during special rituals. During my explorations in the hinterland, I have stumbled upon these stone deities myself and been shown others, but I will not disclose their location since, sadly, a heritage that had remained untouched for centuries is now getting stolen by antique smugglers.

Goan hero-stones—stone panels that usually tell the story of a villager who lost his life in battle or died protecting his village—suffer a similar fate. A number of them depict naval battles. They are worshipped in the open, often near a tribal or village temple. Some beautiful pieces from the Kadamba period (AD 950–1300) are exhibited in the Archaeological Museum in Old Goa.[24] One of the most beautiful hero-stones from the Kadamba period disappeared from the village of Nagvem (Sattari taluka) in 2010. Locally known as Veer Gal, this stone was worshipped by the nomadic Gauli community and depicted a poignant funeral scene showing the hero's corpse on a pyre, with his wife about to commit sati.[25] Luckily, villagers are now becoming alert to this

---

23 A closer analysis of some of these deities, such as the unique Goan goddesses in boats, has been provided by Pratima P. Kamat, *Goa, Its Tryst with Trade*, pp. 129–33.

24 See Sila Tripati, 'Ships on Hero Stones from the West Coast of India' [http://drs.nio.org/drs/bitstream/2264/180/1/IJNA-%20Herostones-%202006%2035%20(1).pdf].

25 The stolen Veer Gal was later found in the forest, broken into four pieces. See 'Mystery continues over missing 13th century Hero Stone in Goa', in *Deccan Herald,* 10 March 2011 (http://www.deccanherald.com/content/144652/mystery-continues-over-missing-13th.html).

threat. Recently the people of Bhuipal (Sattari), foiled an attempt by antique smugglers to steal the hero-stone that they worship at Khetmachegalav.

Driving through the hinterland of south Goa, I once caught sight of a magnificent white champa tree in bloom. I stopped the car to admire the tree and discovered near it a small temple with Paik and some other tribal gods within it. Next to it was a hero-stone. The 'eco-theological synergy' (to use Manoj R. Borkar's phrase) that is such an integral part of the culture of the hinterland communities, ensured that this spot remained pristine. This also underlined for me the importance of preserving the traditions of these hinterland communities that have so uniquely enriched Goa's culture and environment.

Recently there has been some talk of declaring one of these hinterland areas—the Madhei wildlife sanctuary—a tiger reserve. Tigers in Goa? one may wonder. They have indeed been sighted here, most recently in 2011. There are also leopards, Malabar giant squirrels and hornbills in Goa's forested hinterland, yet there has been remarkably little interest in developing these areas for wildlife tourism. Perhaps this is because other wildlife sanctuaries not so far away, such as the amazing Kabini wildlife sanctuary near Bangalore, have more to offer. Some experts argue that Goa is a tiger corridor and doesn't have a breeding tiger population. More conclusive evidence is needed before a decision to declare the Madhei sanctuary as a tiger reserve can be taken. But meanwhile, mining interests stand in the way of creating a tiger reserve in Goa,[26] since this would mean that all

---

26 See 'Tigers in Goa', in *Herald*, 15 May 2012 (http://oheraldo.in/ newpage.php?month=5&day=15&year=2012&catid=15); see also

open mining in that area would have to stop. Mining has been destroying Goa's hinterland and since that is a story that reads like a crime thriller, I have dedicated a whole chapter to it.

'Water Security Under Threat If Mining Increases', in *Times of India*, 1 November 2011 (http://articles.timesofindia.indiatimes.com/2011-11-01/goa/30345206_1_mining-leases-excessive-mining-mining-belt).

12

The Curse of the Red Gold Rush

Emerald-green fields dotted with coconut groves, forested hillsides yielding to flourishing cashew plantations—that used to be the idyllic landscape of south Goa and its hinterland, born of its rich red earth. Alas, that rich red earth has, over the past few years, spelt doom and destruction for the environment and the people of this area.

Only very few resist temptations and threats connected to the red gold rush. Take, for example, Cheryl D'Souza, a Goan woman in her mid-forties who lives on a farm in the village of Maina in south Goa. She grew up in East Africa and returned to her homeland with her husband nearly twenty years ago. Together they bought 240 acres of farmland in Maina to live out their dream. A Goa minister had also bought 2 lakh square metres of land in the village and started threatening neighbours to sell their plots to him, which they did, so he could exploit the land and get rich through mining. Their fields were bulldozed, the forests were cut down and the red earth deeply scarred as the minister's mining operations got under way. But one person who refused to sell, despite being offered crores of rupees, was Cheryl. Then, in 2006, Cheryl's husband died in a tragic accident—he was electrocuted while helping a neighbour carry out repairs. After that, the threatening night-time calls of the mining mafia began, for Cheryl's farmland sat on a gold mine of huge deposits of first-grade iron ore.[1] As a lone woman, she could now be pressured to sell her land, they thought. 'Do you know what can happen to a woman alone at night?'/'Your daughter is so pretty, aren't you afraid of what might happen to her?'/'Your problem is, no man has taught you a lesson yet.'[2] They underestimated this stubborn and fearless woman who told the journalist Aimee Ginsburg, 'I am not going to walk out. They will only get the land over my dead body.'[3]

'She is a tough cookie, a pretty good fighter,' says Claude Alvares, who, together with his wife, Norma, runs the Goa Foundation, a small but powerful NGO dedicated to the protection of Goa's environment. And indeed, Cheryl has set an example that most others in her situation would find hard to emulate. She placed her own principles, as well as environmental concerns, higher than her personal profit—she would have been a billionaire if she had not resisted being 'bought out' with the unbelievable sum of Rs 70 crore.

Goa has a long history of being exploited for personal gain by those in power. The *Estado da Índia* in the sixteenth century was 'a happy hunting ground for the dishonest and the unscrupulous', with the Portuguese viceroys themselves looking at their office as a three-year-long opportunity to 'harvest and carry off the fruit' of the lands that they administered, writes the well-known historian Pratima Kamat.[4] That tradition of institutionalized corruption in

---

1 Aimee Ginsburg, 'And She Wore Iron', in *Outlook*, 23 May 2011 (http://www.outlookindia.com/article.aspx?271812).

2 Ibid.

3 Ibid.

4 Pratima P. Kamat, Goa, *Its Tryst with Trade* (Panaji: Goa Chamber of Commerce and Industry, 2009), p. 157.

Goa continues to thrive. Indeed, politicians and ministers today are more than a match for their Portuguese predecessors, apparently subscribing to the maxim of *nay virra kachi kulaikkatu* (money is unconcerned with the means through which it is obtained).[5]

Corruption in Goa is not restricted to the mining sector, but seeps into all realms of life and sometimes takes amusing forms. Take, for example, the sub-inspector who was in charge of the Anti-Narcotics Cell (ANC) in Goa. When it surfaced in January 2011 that twenty-four kilograms of *charas* (cannabis)—around 10 per cent of the confiscated drugs in the police storeroom—had gone missing, he feigned surprise. Unfortunately for him, a video was uploaded on the net showing him selling drugs to two foreign tourists, a simple way of pushing drugs seized by the ANC back into the narcotics market. He did not know how to get out of this uncomfortable situation till an ingenious solution came to him: he made an official declaration that the missing drugs in the storeroom must have been eaten by white ants. Terror of the tropics, these tiny termites eat their way through wood, paper, roof rafters and mud walls. White ants once ate through not only a bookshelf in our house, but also my jeans! If they had indeed eaten kilos of confiscated cannabis from the police storeroom, they must still be dancing merrily in heaven. The police sub-inspector was suspended shortly after the discovery that the cannabis was missing, but the case was handed to the CBI only seven months later, in July 2011—giving him enough time to destroy all the

5 See *Socio-Economic Aspects of Portuguese Colonialism in Goa: 19th and 20th Centuries*. Edited by B.S. Shastry. (Belgaum: Yarbal Printers, 1990), p. 209.

evidence. So, in all probability, he will be acquitted.[6] In another case, now under investigation, the son of Goa's former home minister was charged with allegedly sheltering Goa's drug mafia, and playing a major role in their operations.[7]

In April 2011, Goa's minister of education, himself a school dropout, was caught taking more than Rs 1 crore in cash and cheques out to Dubai (his son, by the way, is accused of having raped a fourteen-year-old German girl).[8] Goa's chief minister at the time dismissed his minister's behaviour as a small, unimportant matter. Another case concerns Goa's civil supplies minister, who was allegedly involved in a fake-currency racket, whereby counterfeit notes, sourced from Bangladesh, were being pumped into a casino in Goa that was busted in August 2011. 'Why should I be afraid?' he is reported to have asked.[9] And he

6 See 'Ravi Orders Probe into ANC Goings-on', in *Times of India*, 15 April 2010 (http://articles.timesofindia.indiatimes.com/2010-04-15/goa/28138699_1_police-storehouse-white-ants-charas); 'Ants "Ate" 24 Kg Drugs: Prosecution Tells Court', in IBN Live (http://ibnlive.in.com/news/ants-ate-24-kg-drugs-prosecution-tells-cou/113314-3.html).

7 See 'Crime: A Pathetic Inheritance of the Past', in *The Goan*, 9 March 2013 (http://www.thegoan.net/Goa/News/Crime-A-pathetic-inheritance-of-the-past/03382.html).

8 See 'Minister Caught with Rs 1 Crore', in Times Now (http://www.youtube.com/watch?v=kS283zulrnk); 'Goa Education Minister Detained at Mum Airport' in IBN Live (http://ibnlive.in.com/news/goa-education-minister-detained-at-mum-airport/148022-3.html).

9 See 'Accused in Counterfeit Currency a Regular Visitor of Goa Minister,' in Goa4U, 12 August 2011 (http://goa4u.com/2011/08/12/accused-in-counterfeit-currency-a-regular-visitor-of-goa-minister/); Daijiworld, 'Fake Currency Racket Reaches Goa Minister's Doorstep', in Daijiworld.com, 11 August 2011 (http://www.daijiworld.com/news/news_disp.asp?n_id=111690).

is right. If you have political clout or connections to the political class, such cases never end in conviction or punishment. No wonder those involved in mining, flouting environmental laws and regulations and destroying Goa's environment, have managed to function with impunity.

I have visited south Goa's mining belt several times. On one of my visits to Caurem, the village neighbouring Cheryl D'Souza's, I met the tribal activist Nilesh Gaonkar who has faced a brutal assault in retaliation to his efforts to stop mining (more about Nilesh later in this chapter). I also met Rama Velip from Colomba, a village which, at its peak, had twenty-three open mines that had destroyed the land and livelihood of the villagers. Velip, president of the Bharat Mukti Morcha, told me how the police harass and even arrest villagers if they oppose mining. Over 600 police cases have been filed in the past few years against Colomba villagers alone.[10]

I have been to many other villages affected by open mining, mainly inhabited by tribal communities—Velips, as well as Kunbis and Gowdas—with large settlements in south Goa. It gave me tremendous pain to see how this beautiful area now lies devastated. Agricultural fields and waterbodies have been destroyed through mining silt, trees have been wantonly felled, leaving behind red scars of naked earth. Since thousands of trucks in the mining areas speed through the villages towards Sanvordem and other places to load the soil on to barges for transportation to the

---

10 See 'Rama Velip Harassment by Goa Police Is a Brahmanical Conspiracy to Destroy Self-Reliant Leadership of Scheduled Tribes in Goa', in Bharat Mukti Morcha, 26 July 2012 (http://bharatmukti.blogspot.in/2012/07/rama-velip-harassment-by-goa-police-is.html).

harbour, the traffic is unruly and chaotic, leading to an average of a death a day.[11]

This massive volume of traffic also affects the health of the people thanks to air pollution from the iron-ore dust. Asthma is on the rise and, wherever one looks, trees and plants are covered with a thin layer of the deadly red dust. The degeneration of the quality of life in these areas is all too visible. A report of Forest Minister Felipe Neri Rodrigues reveals that 1314 hectares of forest land—which would add up to around 60,000 trees—has been destroyed over the past four years for non-forest purposes, mainly mining.[12]

The worst-affected talukas are Bicholim in the north, and Sanguem and Quepem in the south. Most of the south Goan mines came up in 2006 and after. Earlier, its soil was of no interest to miners, because south Goa possesses mainly low-grade iron ore (below 58 per cent). But, as Claude Alvares told me, the price of iron ore exploded with the 2008 Beijing Olympics and its huge demand for steel. A ton of iron ore that earlier fetched 15 dollars on the international market was now worth 75 dollars and at times even went up to 180 dollars, before the price settled at 114–120 dollars per ton in 2012. Thus, when the China boom started in 2005–06, all the Dagobert Ducks of Goa's greedy political class were up and running to buy land in south Goa. 'Every red rock in Goa,' writes Vivek Menezes, 'suddenly became equivalent to a

---

11 Paper by Claude Alvares, 'Basic facts on mining leases in Goa', Goa Foundation, 20 July 2012.

12 See 'Since '08 Goa Lost 1,314 Hectares of Forest Land', in *Times of India*, 24 March 2011 (http://articles.timesofindia.indiatimes.com/2011-03-24/goa/29182571_1_forest-land-forest-policy-forest-minister).

big wad of cash.'[13] A whopping 54 million tons of iron ore were exported in 2010–11, more than three times the amount six years earlier. Around 50 per cent of India's total export of iron ore comes from its smallest state which covers less than 1 per cent of India's total land mass.

But the mining boom has extracted a heavy price—Goa's natural riches, such as its springs and forests, are being irreversibly destroyed for the benefit of a few politicians and their industrialist–businessmen cronies. Although I have heard arguments that Goa owes most of its colleges and many other philanthropic endeavours to mine owners, the main ambition of these people is to ensure that 'their bank balance is better than that of the state of Goa', as Wendell Rodricks observed on NDTV.[14] And indeed, in 2010, the Sesa Goa mines (by far the largest mining company) had an income of Rs 4224 crore, while the Goan government had a total annual tax income of Rs 4290 crore (of which Rs 900 crore is mining revenue).[15]

It is no surprise, then, that mining, which started in the 1940s in the last decades of Portuguese rule, got the nickname 'the red gold rush'. For the Portuguese colonial government, revenue from mining came in most handy to pay for imported food and luxury goods at the time of the Indian blockade, shortly before the Liberation. Initially, the Portuguese gave concession for 791

13 Vivek Menezes, 'Goa 2061: Threats, Challenges, Opportunities'. *Libertação 1961–2011*. Edited by Vivek Menezes, p. 148.
14 'Goa's Mining Scam', NDTV, 28 September 2011 (http://www.youtube.com/watch?v=L0N5HredipE&feature=related).
15 Conversation with Claude Alvares, Goa Foundation, 2 February 2012; see also, The Goa Foundation press release (http://goafoundation.org/wp-content/uploads/2009/06/Press-Release-Mining.pdf).

mines, of which 591 were cancelled in 1987, though 336 leases were renewed under Indian law.

An estimated ninety to 100 mines had been operating in the state during the last few years; the Goa Foundation managed to win enough court cases to bring down the number to fifty-eight as of 2012. This number does not, however, include the many illegal mines where the soil is dug up without any government approval whatsoever. But if one takes a closer look at even the so-called 'legal mines', it becomes evident that most of them are actually involved in illegal business. Claude and Norma Alvares have challenged the mining companies to name just one mine that follows all the rules and regulations of the state, but no one has taken up the challenge so far.[16]

Let me illustrate, through one example, some of the shady activities of 'legal mining' during the China boom, when closed or unused leases suddenly began to be operated by people who did not own the original leases. This is a 'legal' (i.e. government-approved) mine in Rivona, a village tucked away in the hinterland, just a forty-minute drive from my house. I first came to Rivona many years back in search of two ancient Buddhist caves. It is a quiet village near the famous Damodar temple in Zambaulim, which is home to a deity rescued and brought here when its main temple in Margao was destroyed in 1565. Rivona village, consisting of only a few houses, is believed to have been home to Buddhist

---

16 None, for example, has clearance from the National Board of Wildlife. Practically all mines operate in a 10-km zone in violation of the Supreme Court's order dated 4 December 2006 without a no-objection certificate from the Standing Committee of the National Board of Wildlife, but the state government refuses to cooperate. See Claude Alvares, 'Basic facts on mining leases in Goa'.

monks who lived and preached here in the sixth or seventh century AD, and the two caves date to that period. On paper, this particular 'legal' mine in Rivona shows someone's name claiming ownership of the mine, while in reality, that mine is owned by one of the wealthiest Goans, who also is a former MLA of the state. To add to the confusion, the mine is operated by a third person, who was a mining contractor well before his entry into politics, when he became a minister in the last government. Owners outsourcing their mines without getting permission from the central government move in a 'grey zone' and their involvement in politics and their high connections ensure that those grey areas continue to thrive.[17]

Local NGOs, the most vocal of them being the Goa Foundation, have been fighting against the mining mafia for the past twenty-one years (the first case was filed in 1992), filing public interest litigations and lawsuits one after another, supporting village activists, being involved in public hearings in affected villages and so on. The Goa Foundation has continued to take the time-consuming and difficult route of public interest litigations, since it is a very effective tool. The massive destruction of wildlife and the environment does not happen because of insufficient regulations and laws—Indian laws are exemplary in this regard—but because of their lack of implementation. Through filing public interest litigations, Norma and Claude Alvares have achieved successes no protests or road blockades can ever achieve. For example, they were once able to close nineteen mines in one shot because these were operating without the consent of the Pollution Control Board under the Water and Air

17 'Goa's Mining Scam', NDTV.

(Prevention and Control of Pollution) acts. However, their crusade involves hours of painstaking work to build well-documented cases and deal with follow-ups, often for months or years, which explains why there is hardly anyone else fighting this tough battle. Claude and Norma, the latter a lawyer by profession, have put in twenty-five years of free service to save their state from being ravaged. 'The government has been completely without scruples in manipulating laws, judges, affidavits,' says Claude. 'They have a whole team of people to only work on that.' This couple is indeed engaged in a lifelong David versus Goliath fight. And despite many setbacks, they have achieved a great deal. They have filed by far the maximum number of cases against the mining industry, and gathered a lot of solid evidence on illegalities. Their biggest triumph came in October 2012, when in response to a petition filed by them, the Supreme Court imposed a ban on all mining in Goa until a committee specially set up by the Centre investigated the case and submitted its report and recommendations.

This development was widely hailed in Goa by all except those with vested interests, because public opinion against the harm caused by mining had been building up steadily. In 2011, open mining in Goa became a political issue, contributing to the fall of the former government and forcing the new one to investigate illegal mining and encroachment into Goa's forest cover, putting severe pressure on politicians involved in the business. The consequences of mining, which the Goa Foundation and other activists have highlighted, have finally shaken the public conscience: deforestation, land degradation, ground- and surface-water contamination, destruction of agricultural land and dust pollution have become issues that now draw active participation from the people of Goa.

In the spring of 2011, the anger of villagers, who, among other things, had lost their paddy and chilli crops because of polluted water and silt in their fields, led to an uprising of (mainly) tribals in south Goa. It was an unprecedented protest which led to the sealing of a mine. Groups of villagers blocked roads and entrances of mines for more than two and a half months in Caurem. Hundreds of trucks, usually overloaded with iron ore, could not leave the mines. Despite facing all kinds of hardships and threats, the villagers eventually succeeded in getting one of the illegal mines—it was destroying an adjacent hill, which was considered to be a sacred grove where Velips would not even break a twig—to shut down. I saw the damage done to the hill—half of it was already gone. Another successful protest recently took place against Sesa Goa's coke plant in Navelim in north Goa, which had to close down in August 2012.

Caurem, the village that challenged the mining industry, is a shocking example of how fast open mining is destroying Goa's environment. Open mining is carried out by cutting trenches into the hilltop or slopes, extending the pits in stages, often going below the water table. It is not just iron ore, but also manganese and bauxite that are mined in Goa. All that is needed are a few machines, a team of labourers to dig the soil and some trucks. Despite these inexpensive operations that bring in profits on an astronomical scale, the owners are too stingy to invest in safety measures for the labourers, which has led to several serious accidents.

I returned to the south Goan mining belt in the first quarter of 2012. When I took photographs of an illegal mine that a young anti-mining activist, Nilesh Gaonkar, had shown me, I was chased by security guards employed there, who even noted down my car number.

Heavy mining in the village of Caurem and its surroundings, as Nilesh explained, started only in 2008, when five mines encircled this tribal village known for its fresh-water springs. There has been a spate of attacks on those who have tried to save their livelihood from the mining menace. Nilesh was brutally attacked with iron rods in May 2011. Repeatedly threatened by the mining goons, he stopped going to work on his bike, lest they stage an 'accident', and started taking the bus instead. One morning, while disembarking from the bus at the Verna Industrial Estate where he worked as an engineer, he was attacked. They did not hit him on the head or spine—the attack was only meant to scare him into silence. Because of the injuries on his arm and shoulder, he could not work for months and ended up losing his job. The assault, however, did not scare off or silence this courageous twenty-four-year-old. He now works full-time as an anti-mining activist.

Like Cheryl, Nilesh is determined to fight on. 'For generations, our forefathers had plenty of water due to the many natural mineral springs,' he says. 'But now, because of mining, we face water-related problems.' Mining operations need huge quantities of fresh water, sucking all the nearby springs dry. We walked to a spring that provides the village with drinking water. The gush of crystal-clear water flowing out of the hill is used for agriculture as well. The whole village of Caurem depends on agriculture, but no one in the mining business is bothered that the prized chilli crop failed for the second time in a row. Cashew flowers have been reduced to half the expected output and paddy no longer grows here, its saplings killed by the mining waste that flows into the fields and chokes all vegetation.

Extracting a ton of iron ore leaves behind 2.5 to 3 tons of mining waste. Such an enormous quantity of waste—100–150 million tons of waste was generated in 2011—causes severe environmental problems.[18] Miners simply pump the muddy slime out of the working pits where operations have gone below the water table. During the four months of Goa's monsoon, the waste dumped around the mine is washed into rivers, fields and waterbodies, degrading the soil and making paddy growth impossible.

To appease the villagers of Caurem, mining companies poured in more than Rs 1 crore to build a new temple, which was almost finished when I saw it in 2012. It was just a stone's throw from the old structure. As I sat with Nilesh under the roof of the old temple, he pointed to the fancy new building and said, 'The god will not move there. We don't want this temple.'

The powerful mining lobby claims that mining brings development, such as infrastructure, to the most backward regions of Goa and provides employment. Mining companies claim to 'reforest' exploited areas with a monoculture of fast-growing eucalyptus trees to replace the thriving biodiversity of hundreds of species. When I flew into Goa recently, I was shocked at the aerial view of mammoth craters, abandoned mine pits and dug-up hills of Goa's red soil, which looked like large, bleeding wounds on a once-pristine land. The Supreme Court's decision to shut down the entire Goan mining industry until strict controls are put in place has not come a moment too soon.

There is a joke regarding the political class that I heard in Goa. It says, the government should consider changing the national emblem from the Lion Capital of Ashoka to a condom, because it more accurately reflects the government's attitude: a condom

---

18 Conversation with Claude Alvares, Goa Foundation, 2 February 2012.

allows inflation, halts production, destroys the next generation, protects a bunch of dicks and gives you a sense of security while you are actually being screwed. . . .

13

Visiting the Migrant Gods

Goa's boundaries today are not what they were when the Portuguese conquered it in 1510. It was only later, in the eighteenth century, that they added what they called the 'new conquests', extending their territories to include Goa's hinterland and mining belt. This explains why so much of the original Hindu and tribal culture survives in these areas.

The territory first occupied by the Portuguese was known as *Ilhas* (the islands), since it was encircled by the arms of the Zuari and Mandovi rivers. The Ilhas comprised the island of Divar, together with Chorao, Jua and Tiswadi, and this formed only a tenth of Goa's present territory. Divar was at that time a pilgrimage hub for the whole of the Konkan region, acknowledged as such even by the Portuguese, who found that 'Divar was as much venerated by the Hindus as the Holy Land is by us'.[1] The destruction of its approximately 160 temples, which began as early as 1540[2], was just the beginning of what was to come in the Portuguese-controlled areas.

Even before the beginning of the Inquisition in 1560, any expression of faith other than Christian was forbidden and

1 Maurice Hall, *Window on Goa* (London: Quiller Press, 1992), p. 108.
2 Anthony D'Costa, 'The Demolitions of the Temples in the Island of Goa in 1540 and the Disposal of Temple Lands'. *Neue Zeitschrift für Missionswissenschaft* (Beckenried, 1962), Vol. 18, p. 163.

punishable. Things got worse after the Inquisition began. For Goan Hindus, who had not left the state in the first fifty years of Portuguese occupation, it now became illegal to worship their gods even behind closed doors, in their homes. Already, in 1549, the governor of Portuguese India, George Cabral, banned the erection of temples and mosques in Portuguese territory and no conversion was permitted except to Christianity.[3] Hindus were not allowed to host marriages, celebrate festivals or cremate their dead. These new decrees were intended to break the spirit (and thus the influence) of the Hindu upper castes, so that Christianity could flourish.[4] The Jesuits, known to be rather militant in their crusade for conversion in the sixteenth century, were especially zealous in helping to enforce these harsh laws.

Such laws arose from a deep frustration on the part of the Christian missionaries, who found that the process of conversion was proving to be much more difficult than what they had anticipated. Many records from the sixteenth and seventeenth centuries testify to the problems the Portuguese faced in Christianizing 'the heathens'.[5] The Italian Jesuit Niccolo Lancilotto remarked during his visit to Goa, 'There are no more temples in [Divar] island . . . but there remains an infinite number of Moors, gentiles and bad Christians.'[6] The 'bad Christians' he

3 Jeanette Pinto, *Slavery in Portuguese India (1510–1842)* (Bombay: Himalaya Publishing House, 1992), p. 67.
4 Manohar Malgonkar, *Inside Goa* (Bardez: Architecture Autonomous, 2004, 1982), p. 34.
5 P. Axelrod/M.A. Fuerch, 'Flight of the Deities: Hindu Resistance in Portuguese Goa'. *Modern Asian Studies* (Cambridge: Cambridge University Press, May 1996) Vol. 30(2), p. 410.
6 Alexander Henn, 'Pictorial Encounter: Iconoclasm and Syncretism on

refers to were converts who had reverted to their original faith or who continued with forbidden practices and idol worship—an indication that conversion was usually motivated not by faith, but by more pragmatic factors, such as economic advantages or the threat of losing possessions and privileges. As Lancilotto writes in a letter dated October 1547, 'The people of this country who become Christians do so purely for temporal advantage, as is inevitable in a land where slavery reigns. Slaves of the Moors or Hindus seek baptism in order to secure their manumission at the hands of the Portuguese . . . The man who embraces the faith from honest conviction is regarded a fool.'[7]

The Portuguese colonial administration found it hard to control the constant resistance they were facing from the people. It was for this reason, to bring the 'bad Christians' in line and wipe out all heresy, that the Inquisition was initiated. It is worth noting that the much-venerated Spanish priest Francis Xavier (disciple of the founder of the Jesuit order, Ignatius Loyola) was the actual initiator of the Goan Inquisition, which lasted more than 250 years until 1812, instigating terror among the people. It was one of the most brutal and long-lasting inquisitions suffered by any country at the time. And yet Francis Xavier remains by far the most revered saint for Goans today—thousands flock to the Basilica of Bom Jesus during his annual feast to have a glimpse of his mummified body, unaware of his role in the Inquisition.

The Palace of Inquisition with its 200 cells, which was called

---

India's Western Coast'. *Transcultural Turbulences*. Edited by C. Brosius and R. Wenzlhuemer (Berlin/Heidelberg: Springer-Verlag, 2011), pp. 153–70.

7 Anant K. Priolkar, *The Goa Inquisition* (Bombay: Bombay University Press, 1961), p. 55.

Santa Casa (holy house) by the Portuguese and Orlem Goro (big house) by the locals, was set up in one of the great plazas in front of the cathedral dedicated to Saint Catherine in Old Goa.[8] Nothing remains of it now and no sign marks this historic site. It must have been one of the most feared places of its time. Most prisoners were Catholics. Although the Inquisition officially was not allowed to prosecute members of other faiths, convicted Hindus also disappeared into the Orlem Goro, their homes burned and salt sprinkled in their fields.

The Inquisition was a means to discipline the heretics of the Christian faith, enforce 'right conduct' through fear and thus turn people forcibly into 'good Catholics'. Torture and death in the Orlem Goro were common, as the accounts of the Inquisition by the Frenchman Charles Dellon, who was a prisoner himself in the seventeenth century, reveal. The climax was the Auto da fé (Act of Faith), at times held annually, at times after a period of a few years, where converted Catholics who refused to confess to misdemeanours or transgressed a second time by holding fast to forbidden rituals and activities were burned publicly at the stake. The Inquisition, which so conveniently served as a tool of colonial hegemony by the Portuguese (and was also used by some to exterminate their rivals),[9] only ended due to British pressure in the nineteenth century, when British troops were actually stationed on Goan soil, threatening to take over.

However, concepts imposed by fear and threats alone could not possibly have survived for centuries to produce the deep-

---

8 Ibid., p. 56.
9 Sr Emma Maria A.C., *Women in Portuguese Goa (1510–1835)* (Tellicherry: Irish, 2002), p. 54.

rooted Christian ethic and faith that is so evident in Goa today.[10] Catholicism as practised in Goa now no longer evokes any memories of its cruel past, and the Church and its institutions are now widely appreciated and respected for the many admirable services they provide to the public. But to go back to the days of the Inquisition—its rigid laws to establish Catholicism and expel Hindus from their homeland was not just a cultural suppression, but an economic and political suppression too: Hindus could not hold public offices, they could not participate in the annual auctions for agricultural *comunidade* land, they were not permitted to ride on horses, in a palanquin, or even wear shoes in public. These restrictions clearly aimed at a deep humiliation, to crack the Hindu pride.[11] There were even dress codes for women, enforced by a decree in April 1736, which forbade them from wearing a *choli* or using *tilak* and *kumkum*.[12]

The cultural, economic and political suppression of anyone who refused to convert led to an exodus in the sixteenth and seventeenth centuries, with the result that Goa slid into an economic crisis: agricultural labour, carpenters, blacksmiths and other craftsmen disappeared and there was a short supply of manpower. Even food had to be imported because of labour shortage.[13] The Portuguese soon learned that it was counterproductive to push the influential Hindus out—trade in Goa was in their hands and the Portuguese depended on their networks. So the administration constantly had to bend its own

---

10 Maurice Hall, *Window on Goa*, p. 6.
11 Arun Sinha, *Goa Indica: A Critical Portrait of Postcolonial Goa* (Delhi: Promilla Publication, 2002), p. 24.
12 Sr Emma Maria A.C., *Women in Portuguese Goa*, p. 108.
13 Arun Sinha, *Goa Indica*, p. 26.

rules to keep the economy going. A telling and hilarious example of this is the absurd *shendi* tax. The *sonars* (jeweller caste) of Goa, almost exclusively Hindu, were 'too valuable a community to drive out'.[14] They were permitted to live as Hindus in Christian areas and even keep their caste symbol, the shendi, which is a kind of thin ponytail at the crown of the head. As a compromise, they were simply asked to pay a heavy tax of three xeraphims (gold *mohurs*) on their shendi, a tax that lasted for 300 years, till it was finally abolished in December 1840.[15]

In the climate of fear provoked by the Inquisition, religious rituals had to be performed in secret. Idols of gods and goddesses were made of paper, so that they could easily be destroyed during a raid or after the ritual was over. The practice of using paper cut-outs as idols still survives in some Goan Hindu families, such as the Mamai Kamats in Panjim, who worship a picture of the elephant god during the Ganesh Chaturthi festival, instead of the usual clay statue.[16] The most difficult rite to perform in secret was the cremation of the dead, which is so fundamental to the Hindu religion. Yet this too continued clandestinely:[17] death in a Hindu household was kept secret and the cremation done under the cover of darkness, with the dead body placed on a boat piled with firewood, lit and pushed off into the river. By the time the authorities got to know about it, the boat had travelled far, so most of the time it became impossible to locate the family of the deceased.[18]

---

14 Manohar Malgonkar, *Inside Goa*, p. 40.

15 Ibid., pp. 40–1.

16 Ibid., p. 45.

17 Maurice Hall, *Window on Goa*, p. 6.

18 Manohar Malgonkar, *Inside Goa*, p. 45.

These stratagems of the Hindu community and of forcibly converted Christians must have been partly organized, partly spontaneous. But the distinctive manner in which Goan religious festivals are celebrated today is undoubtedly influenced by their historical past. The practice of Goan Catholics and Hindus worshipping together at certain annual festivals, as well as the coinciding of the timing of some of them, is unique to Goa. Many of these festivals are connected to the flight of the gods, when in 1543, the areas of Bardez, Mormugao and Salcete were added to the Portuguese-controlled territory, and the onslaught on Hindu culture spread. Virtually every temple in the old conquests was destroyed. It is striking that the attack on Hindu idols and temples in Goa occurred in the same period as the so-called *Bildersturm* (iconoclasm) in Europe, a wave of destruction of idols and images in Catholic churches and chapels in France, Holland, Germany and other European countries by the Protestants, which reached its climax in the 1560s.[19]

An edict from 1541 gave the viceroy of Goa the authority to demolish any temple or shrine without explanation. This was the time when the migration of Hindu gods and goddesses began. Many idols were destroyed before they could be taken away to safety. It is said that five deities, 'the Village Five', formed the core of village worship in Goa before the demolition of the temples: they consisted of Shantadurga (in her varied local forms), Lakshminarayana and three forms of Shiva (Ravalnath, originally a folk deity, Bhairava, a fierce form of Shiva, and Betal, who is even fiercer).[20] One still finds their images in villages and forest

---

19 Alexander Henn, *Pictorial Encounter*, pp. 156–7.
20 See Maurice Hall, *Window on Goa*, p. 19.

areas in the hinterland, since these areas were out of reach for the Portuguese in the sixteenth and seventeenth centuries and were only incorporated into Goa in the eighteenth century.

People risked their lives to save the temple idols and smuggle them into neighbouring territories. Take, for example, Goddess Navadurga. Her temple was originally in Karad, from where she was moved to Benaulim and later, when persecuted there, to her current location at Borim. When I visited the goddess on my way to the Siddhanath hill, I met Mr Borkar, a tiny old man with just a few yellow teeth left in his mouth, who was particularly pleased that I, a foreigner from Benaulim (which was the earlier dwelling place of the goddess to whom he is devoted), had come to honour her.

One of the many successful rescues by villagers in Salcete was that of Goddess Kamakshi. I had long wished to visit her temple in Shiroda. So, when in August 2011, I read in the interior design magazine *Inside Outside* about a Goan architect who had built an ultra-modern designer bus terminal in Shiroda (probably to deal with the crowds that pour in during festivals celebrating the goddess), I hopped on to the local bus from Margao to Shiroda, curious to see how such a terminal would fit into the surroundings of this small Goan town.

And thereby hangs another tale, which digresses from the story of the goddess but is typical of Goa. In the photos in the magazine I saw a post-modern structure into which a lot of thought had clearly gone. Even the roof had a connection to the place, having been designed like the wings of Garuda, the mythical eagle who is the mount of not only Vishnu, but also of Goddess Kamakshi. Travelling past paddy fields transformed into a light lush green by the monsoon, enjoying the dazzling sight of white herons called egrets in the overflowing ponds, crossing other buses with names such as 'Praise the Lord', 'Vailankanni' or 'Deep Travels'—all to the accompaniment of loud Hindi pop music—we passed the Zuari river and approached our destination. But to my surprise, we whizzed past the new bus stand, which I recognized instantly from the photos. Instead, the bus driver stopped with shrieking brakes at the Shiroda market half a minute later. I asked him why he did not stop at the new bus terminal. 'No bus stops there,' he responded. 'Why not?' I asked. 'I don't know,' he answered and shrugged his shoulders, smiling widely. Puzzled, I wandered through the Shiroda market, taking in its sights and sounds—a cat sleeping on a pile of *paan* leaves, a shop selling 'Indian Made Foreign Liquor' (I wonder which genius thought up this bizarre term for Indian-made whisky, beer, rum and brandy), a grumpy one-armed woman attending to a noisy mill where spices were being ground, a tea stall where a young man named Vikrant sold me excellent tea. Vikrant informed me that the new bus terminal was nothing but a big scam. Inaugurated in 2008, the Rs 2.5-crore terminal remains deserted, except for a few stray dogs sleeping in its corners. A guard, reading a newspaper in his cubicle, explained, 'Why should any bus leave from there? The market is a much more convenient place.'

Whether it is because of sheer indifference, lack of planning around the needs of a small town and its people, or the anarchy of the common man who simply refuses to accept a project he has no need for, is not for me to decide. However, one thing is for sure: the local minister's pockets must have got a substantial refill even as the Garuda on the bus terminal soars unfettered!

I walked on to pay my respects to Goddess Kamakshi, who is housed in an imposing temple not far from the market. Kamakshi, popularly believed to be a form of Parvati, is also regarded as a form of Shantadurga, the Goddess of Peace. Some claim that her main temple is located in Guwahati, Assam, while others say it is in Kanchipuram, Tamil Nadu. It is, however, generally agreed that the goddess showers powerful blessings on anyone who worships her with sincerity. Thus, devotees of all faiths—Hindus, Christians and even Muslims—come here, especially during major festivals, such as Dussehra, Shivaratri, Shigmo or Gokulashtami (Krishna Janmashtami).

In the sixteenth century, when the Kamakshi temple in Raia was about to be destroyed by the feared Captain Diogo Rodrigues, a poor potter from Raia smuggled the idol across the river, hiding it in the village of Shiroda. In memory of the man's courage, the potter community of Raia still enjoys the right to light the lamps at the annual Kamakshi festival. They also supply the numerous clay lamps for the festival, which helps them to earn a living.[21]

Many of the rescued idols in south Goa needed to travel just a few kilometres to be out of Portuguese reach. They only had to cross the Zuari river into Ponda district. The migrant gods were then kept hidden in modest buildings or small huts. They were worshipped not only by their new hosts, but also by other Goans who secretly sneaked back and forth across the border to visit their gods. Their hiding places remained obscure to avert the danger of raids conducted by the Portuguese across the border.[22] Only much later, from the eighteenth century onwards—when the menace of temple destruction had passed—were the impressive shrines

---

21 See http://theflightofgods.wordpress.com/tag/kamakshi-temple-goa/;
   see also Maurice Hall, *Window on Goa*, p. 150.
22 Maurice Hall, *Window on Goa*, p. 21.

one finds today in Ponda, Bicholim and elsewhere erected. I was surprised to learn that more than fifty gods and their temples had found new homes: the Saptakoteshwar temple at Narve was moved from Divar island; the Shantadurga temple changed home from Mapusa to Sanquelem and later to Sawantwadi, till it reached its current location at Dhargar; the Damodar temple at Zambaulim shifted there from Margao; the Shantadurga temple at Fatorpa from Cuncolim; the Mangueshi temple at Mangueshi from Cortalim; the Mahalaxmi temple from Colva found a new home at Bandode; the Shantadurga temple at Kavlem migrated from Kelsi and the Sanusthan Goudpadacharya at Kavlem from Cortalim, to name just a few.

The shrines of the migrant gods I have visited over the years were of special interest to me because Goan temple architecture displays unique characteristics that cannot be seen anywhere else in the country. As pointed out by others, Hindu craftsmen integrated Muslim features and were also influenced by Christian church architecture. Two features of Goan temples are particularly significant and are easily spotted even by an untrained eye: the first is the traditional pyramidal tower or *shikhara* constructed atop the temple sanctuary, which, in Goan shrines, is transformed into a dome resting on an octagonal base or drum; the second is the lamp tower or *deepastambha* that is found in nearly every Goan temple.[23]

Almost all these temples are erected in the Portuguese 'new conquests'. These consist of four southern districts—Ponda, Sanguem, Quepem and Canacona—and three northern districts— Pernem, Bicholim and Sattari. The southern districts were integrated in 1764, when the Raja of Sonda under threat from

---

23 Ibid., p. 21.

Haider Ali of Mysore, fled to Goa and requested the Portuguese to occupy his territory until the threat blew over,[24] while the northern districts were added between 1781 and 1788.[25] Since the policies towards Hinduism were much more relaxed by then, the idols and temples of these new conquests remained untouched, encouraging the Hindu community to extend humble temple structures or erect larger, new temples for the migrant gods in the style described earlier.

It is often forgotten that the migrant gods are closely linked to family lineages in Goa. Goan Hindus can easily figure out to which caste someone with a particular surname belongs by inquiring about his or her family temple. Goans visit their family temples frequently and 'migrant Goans' from other Indian states or abroad make it a point to visit their 'migrant gods' at least once a year. There are even Catholic Goans, such as the Miranda family, who continued for generations to pay their respects annually at the family temple of their Hindu ancestors.

Hinduism and Christianity, Islam and Buddhism, all played a part in shaping Goa's past and present. In the mists of time, Aparanta (one of the many beautiful names by which Goa was known in earlier centuries) was famous as a holy place, part of India's 'sacred geography'. Legend has it that Lord Shiva chose Goa as his place of exile when he lost all his possessions to his wife, Parvati, in a game of dice. She eventually went searching for him and they were reunited in Goa, where they lived for a few million years on the banks of the Zuari river.[26] As mentioned

---

24 Ibid., p. 9.
25 Ibid., p. 9.
26 Ibid., p. 17.

earlier, the holiest place for Hindus was Divar, the small island where residents were forcibly converted to Christianity by the Portuguese in the first half of the sixteenth century.

Goa had a vibrant Muslim community too. The traveller Richard Burton writes, 'We are informed by the Muslim historians that their faith spread wide and took deep roots in the southern parts of Western India, principally in consequence of the extensive immigration of Arabs.'[27] It is believed that the earliest mosque in Goa was built in the eleventh century under the patronage of Jayakeshi I (who also had two Buddhist monks at his court). Later, during the rule of Adil Shah (1490–1510), intermarriage between Muslims and Hindus was common. It was a time when a chain of Muslim commercial settlements spread Muslim power along the Konkan coast.[28] Thus, a Goan Muslim community—a product of local converts, intermarriages and those who were forcibly converted—emerged. Earlier, it was difficult to distinguish Hindu and Muslim communities from their outward appearance. Goa's staple food, fish curry and rice, was the mainstay of all communities alike. That the two cultures merged is also indicated by the term *moplah,* meaning 'son-in-law', that Hindus across the western coast used for Muslims. Today, however, with the increasing influx of Muslim migrants from other states and Wahabi and Salafi influences on Muslims returning to Goa from the Gulf countries, the Muslim community has started to isolate itself. In the ten years we have lived here, we have observed these

---

27 Richard F. Burton, *Goa, and the Blue Mountains* (Santa Barbara: The Narrative Press, 2001), p. 160.

28 V.T. Gune, *Ancient Shrines of Goa,* (Panjim: Government of Goa, Daman and Diu, Dept. of Information, Publications Unit, 1965), p. 4.

changes in our village, Benaulim, where Muslim men have begun to grow long beards and women, who never wore veils, are now fully clad in burkas.

Buddhist and Jain presence in Goa dates back to an earlier era. Buddhist monks lived and taught in Goa from the third century BC onwards and Buddhist as well as Jain settlements were found on trade routes in ancient and early-medieval Goa.[29] The learned monk Dharmarakshita, a Greek convert, was sent by Ashoka to preach in Goa and, according to Buddhist writings in Ceylon (Sri Lanka), the monk Punna was responsible for the spread of Buddhism in Goa at a time when Goa was known as Sunnaparant.[30] The most ancient Buddhist sculpture found in north Goa in the village Colvale dates from the first century AD and is Hellenistic in style.[31] There are traces of Buddhism and Jainism from the pre-colonial period in Colvale, Korgao, the caves of Lamgao, Narve, Kudnem, Kothambi, Bandora, Rivona and Chandor,[32] though detailed documentation is not available.

Sculptures of Jain Tirthankaras were found in the old Kadamba capital of Chandor, in Kudnem, Kothambi and elsewhere. Historian Pratima Kamat writes that the 'present-day Bicholim taluka, through which have passed many trade routes linking the coast with the ghats, exhibits a rich Jain heritage, located in Kothambi and Kudnem, where the remains of a Jain shrine are

29 Pratima P. Kamat, *Goa, Its Tryst with Trade* (Panaji: Goa Chamber of Commerce and Industry, 2009), p. 94, 117.

30 See V.T. Gune, 'Goa's Coastal Overseas Trade', in *Goa through the Ages*. Edited by Teotonio R. de Souza (New Delhi: Concept Publishing Company, 1989, 1999) Vol. II, p. 118.

31 Ibid., p. 119.

32 Pratima P. Kamat, *Goa, Its Tryst with Trade*, p. 118.

still visible.'[33] Subscribing to *ahimsa* or non-violence, the Jain as well as Buddhist communities were largely active in trade, since trade was regarded as the least violent profession. They flourished under the patronage of rich merchants, but their influence in Goa waned between the fifth and eleventh centuries AD,[34] which can also be observed in the alteration of the so-called 'Pandava caves' that are found at different places in Goa. They were originally Buddhist caves, but with the consecration of a *linga*, they were changed by Nathpanthis into Brahminical shrines.[35]

The strong presence of Buddhism and Jainism and their influence in ancient Goa is mainly ignored, often not even known, because most of the remains of this culture have vanished with just a few ruins scattered around the state. Perhaps for this reason, it gave me great pleasure to drive around Goa trying to locate the ruins.

All of this points to a religious tolerance that existed in ancient and early-medieval Goa, and continues today. Hindus, Catholics and Muslims live in parallel communities, which are friendly to each other though not necessarily 'fraternal', as the journalist Arun Sinha observes.[36] What connects these communities is the fact that all of them were at some point *bhailes*, outsiders, set apart from the tribals who are considered the indigenous inhabitants of Goa. They all came to Goa because of its economic opportunities, cultural diversity and geographical beauty—like us, the modern *bhailes*, hailing from other countries or states within India.

---

33 Ibid., p. 122.
34 Ibid., p. 93.
35 Ibid., p. 117.
36 Arun Sinha, *Goa Indica*, chapters 5 and 6.

14

Horses, Slaves and Women

Goa had been a vibrant trading centre long before the Portuguese arrived. Textiles, spices, precious stones and jewellery were among the much-sought-after commodities that sailed in and out of Goa. And so, I was surprised to discover, were horses, which were a major item of Goan trade for centuries.

My great-great-grandfather, a German adventurer and captain, was one of those who knew something about the horse trade with the Indian subcontinent. In 1850, he sailed his ship, the *Virginia*, into Calcutta with 200 horses on board for a local maharaja. He describes in his memoirs how they stored food and water for the animals on the middle deck, and that each horse needed to be strapped into strong belts, so that in rough weather they 'swayed like a hammock'. During the passage, he recounted, the horses were never allowed to lie down, unless they were dying. I wonder how these sensitive animals responded to such a traumatic journey into their unknown future.

The port of Goa, which was directly connected to the trade routes across the Western Ghats, was the most convenient one for Arab merchants to deliver their horses to the Vijayanagara kings. Because of the many wars with neighbouring kingdoms, Vijayanagara's demand for cavalry horses was insatiable.

The trade in Arabian horses, which accounted for half of Goa's revenues at one time, now seems to have faded from local memory. In the sixteenth century, when the Portuguese defeated the Arabs, they took over the lucrative horse trade in Goa. Afonso de Albuquerque, the conqueror of Goa, dispatched sea patrols to enforce Portuguese monopoly of the horse trade all along the western coast, giving the traders no option but to unload their equine cargo at the port of Goa. In order to encourage the horse trade and gain from its revenues, the Portuguese decreed that any ship that brought at least ten horses to Goa was exempt from paying customs duty on the rest of its cargo.[1]

Because of its immense economic importance, 'trading vessels going to Hormuz to buy horses, had to leave behind a surety in Goa to guarantee their return to the same port with their precious cargo'.[2] Arab steeds were imported from countries of West Asia as well as Afghanistan, in exchange for calico, muslin, rice, sugar, iron, areca nut, pepper, ginger, spices and medicines through the old Goan port of Gopakapattana located on the Zuari river, and later, when Gopakapattana was silted up after a flood in the twelfth century, through the new port of Ella, which today, is Goa Velha. The demand for horses for the cavalries of Indian rulers was so high that the countries breeding the animals did not have enough grass to feed them. So grass, which grew aplenty in Goa, used to be exported to West Asia.[3] Historical sources reveal that great care was taken to ensure 'that those who dealt with horses were provided requisite amenities in terms of

1 M.N. Pearson, *Coastal Western India: Studies from the Portuguese Records* (New Delhi: Concept Publishing Company, 1981), p. 78.
2 Pratima P. Kamat, *Goa, Its Tryst with Trade* (Panaji: Goa Chamber of Commerce and Industry, 2009), p. 177
3 Ibid., p. 18.

housing and provisions, and grass and stables for their horses'.[4]

Recently, I stumbled upon what may be a small surviving vestige of those days when I found an old horse shrine in Usgao, in the hinterland of Goa. In my imagination, Usgao, located on the old trading route, must have been a stopover for horse caravans. Perhaps the horses rested there at night after a long day's march, before being ferried upstream by boat on the Mandovi river to cross the Western Ghats into the Deccan, from where they joined the armies of local and Deccani rulers. The horse shrine I found is built around a banyan tree and villagers still worship it—there are charms hidden in the branches, and flower and coconut offerings around the trunk. The shrine is littered with horse figures in all sizes: clay horses, painted horses, small metal horses. These votive horses, by the way, have nothing in common with the tribal god Paik, mounted on a horse, and worshipped by the Velip community, about whom I have written in Chapter 11. Since people tend to worship what they depend on, I imagine there must once have been a vibrant horse-worship tradition, with many more shrines along the traditional trade routes to the Deccan. Another vestige of this tradition is, as Pratima Kamat suggests, 'the festival of Ghoddemodnni',[5] during which a folk dance represents a horse and its rider setting off for the battlefield. Ghoddemodnni involves horse-like movements and is still performed in a few places in north Goa, especially during the Shigmo festival that usually takes place in March.

Today, there is only one horse farm in Goa, tucked away in the lush green landscape at the foot of the Western Ghats, not too far

---

4 Ibid., p.177.
5 Ibid., p. 97.

from my village. Pala Farm, located in Tilamol in Quepem, is run by Monique, a Swiss woman, who has had a passion for horses since childhood. With her husband, Nazir, she decided to live her dream, and bought a few beautiful horses from Rajasthan. The animals are trained and cared for by her, and roam around freely on her property. Apart from Monique and Nazir's thirteen happy animals, and a few tired and sad-looking ponies that carry children up and down the beach at Majorda, I have never spotted horses anywhere else in Goa. Horses and the horse trade have vanished from the landscape, as well as from the Goans' collective memory.

Today, Usgao's horse caravans have been replaced by mining trucks belching diesel fumes and stirring up clouds of toxic dust, their bellies filled with iron ore from the mines. I can't help but compare the economics of the horse caravans to that of the modern mining caravans: both brought immense riches to the state as well as the traders. But while the horse caravans brought prosperity to people along the trade route, the mining caravans compromise the quality of life and destroy the environment. Horses were the backbone of Goa's prosperity, as mining is today, and a heavy tax was levied on each of them. Indeed, the tax shelled out for a horse imported into Goa was higher than the price paid for an African slave. A steed could be sold for as much as 800 pardaus, and its tax to the state was 42 pardaus,[6] while the most expensive slave, according to the writings of the French traveller François de Pyrard, cost around 20 to 30 pardaus.

~

---

6 Ibid., p. 76.

Nevertheless, the slave trade also brought riches to Goa, and slaves and horses were regularly auctioned in its markets. The most famous of these was the Rua Direita, also known as the Rua dos Leiloes, the street of auctions.[7] Today, unfortunately, there are no signboards in Old Goa to point out such historic landmarks, but it is known for a fact that the Rua Direita was in front of the Se Cathedral. It is recorded that slaves were even sold at the doorstep of the Se Cathedral and the viceroy's palace.[8] Many slaves owned by the government were made to work in the ships' galleys, while slaves owned by the Portuguese and by locals mainly did domestic work, the women also serving as concubines to their masters. Every time I visit Old Goa to show visiting friends around, my inner eye projects images of a bustling bazaar, haggling traders and groups of shackled slaves.

Though slavery has existed in many countries, whether in Egypt, India, Rome, the Muslim world or the United States of America, the African slave trade is the story of white people discovering and cruelly exploiting the 'dark continent'.[9] The trade in African slaves assumed immense proportions under the Portuguese, even before they set foot in India, and they were among the nations that profited the most from the slave trade.[10] They earned huge revenues in gold, transporting slaves from one trading post to another along the Atlantic coast of Africa, selling

---

7 Ibid., p. 156.
8 Fatima de Silva Gracias, *Kaleidoscope of Women in Goa, 1510–1961* (New Delhi: Concept Publishing Company, 1996), p. 46.
9 Jeanette Pinto, *Slavery in Portuguese India (1510–1842)* (Mumbai: Himalaya Publishing House, 1992), p. 3.
10 Ibid., pp. 10–11, 96.

them to Muslim merchants.[11] As C.R. Boxer has observed, the number of slaves captured in Africa between 1450 and 1500 by the Portuguese was as high as 150,000.[12] In the sixteenth century, with the discovery of India and the establishment of sugar plantations, a new market for the slave trade emerged and Goa was one of its main ports, connecting it 'not just with Mocambique, but also French Mauritius, Macau and Ceylon. Such human cargoes were handled by Goan merchants such as the Mhamai Kamat brothers who had served as brokers and agents for the French'.[13] The Goa municipality even had a slave retriever in its service, to capture runaway slaves, as Teotonio R. de Souza has discovered from historical records.[14]

However, the majority of Goans today express total ignorance of the slave trade that was so dominant in Goa in the sixteenth and seventeenth centuries, and many deny that it even existed. This, despite the fact that African ancestry is evident in the facial features of many Goans, almost exclusively Catholic and often from the upper class. African slaves were mostly owned by the Portuguese and wealthy locals, and an early-seventeenth-century estimate indicates that each *casado* had around ten slaves.[15] The

---

11 About.com   (http://africanhistory.about.com/od/slavery/ss/Origins_Of_Slave_Trade.htm).

12 C.R. Boxer, *The Portuguese Seaborne Empire, 1415–1825* (London: Hutchinson & Co., 1969), p. 152.

13 Pratima P. Kamat, *Goa, Its Tryst with Trade*, pp. 183, 225.

14 Teotonio R. de Souza, 'Manumission of Slaves in Goa during 1682 to 1760 as Found in Codex 860'. *TADIA—The African Diaspora in Asia: Explorations on a Less Known Fact*. Edited by Kiran Kamal Prasad and Jean-Pierre Angenot (Bangalore: Jana Jagriti Prakashana, 2008), p. 168 (http://www.scribd.com/doc/9503858/African-Slavery-in-Goa).

15 Fatima de Silva Gracias, *Kaleidoscope of Women in Goa*, p. 46.

French navigator François de Pyrard de Laval, who visited Goa in 1603, writes: 'Among the girls . . . the ones that are preferred are the Kaffir girls from Mozambique who have black skins, woolly hair and are very tall.'[16] In other words, female African slaves—affluent households often had a 'harem' of them—were bought not just to do domestic chores but also to serve as concubines for their owners. Other travellers, such as Linschoten, Pietro della Valle and Gemelli Careri, also testify to the presence of black and mulatto slaves in Goa's households.[17] Officially, non-Christians were not allowed to possess slaves under Portuguese rule, though in practice the ban was not really observed.[18] With this history, it is not surprising that African blood flows through many Goans' veins. There were even regulations to safeguard the offspring of female slaves: a slave who conceived a child by her master could not be sold and the child born was either accepted by its master and his household or considered to be free. A child born to a slave woman gave her also the right to be free after the death of the master.[19]

Though most slaves in Goa were African, there are also records of Japanese slaves brought here in the last quarter of the sixteenth century, as well as slaves from other parts of India and from Goan tribal communities. Quite a few male and female slaves in Goa belonged, for example, to the curumbim (kunbi) caste.[20]

There is another interesting twist regarding the slave trade on India's western coast. The Western Ghat region of Karnataka,

16 Colaco.net (http://www.colaco.net/1/AdmCamoens3.htm)
17 Pratima P. Kamat, *Goa, Its Tryst with Trade*, p. 156.
18 Fatima de Silva Gracias, *Kaleidoscope of Women in Goa*, p. 46.
19 Teotonio R. de Souza, 'Manumission of Slaves in Goa', p. 168.
20 Ibid., p. 176.

Goa's neighbouring state, has been the home of an African community called Siddi for the past 400 years. They live a hand-to-mouth existence as agricultural labourers, often in secluded forest areas, and are the descendants of East African slaves, mainly from Mozambique and Tanzania. It is believed that the Siddis of Karnataka are descendants of freed slaves as well as runaways from Goa, who hid in the forests of North Canara. Today they live mainly around Yellapur, Haliyal, Mundgod, and also in Khanapur in the Belgaum area, while others have migrated to Pakistan. Gujarat also has a sizeable community of Siddis, all of whom are Muslim, though the present-day Siddis of Karnataka can be Hindu, Muslim or Christian. Christian Siddis carry Portuguese names like Pedro, Roberto and Paulo and surnames like Fernandes and Soza.[21] I recently read a report that the Siddis of Karnataka believe that Barack Obama shares their ancestry, and they were keen to gift him a bottle of honey on his visit to India.[22]

The Catholic Church, including orders like the Jesuits, was also involved in the brutal African slave trade in and around Goa. Slaves served in the households of priests, in institutions of charity and in convents. Tellingly, they were entered as 'items' in the account books of Jesuits and others in Portuguese Goa. The Jesuits were not only active in education and their mission to 'save souls', but were also involved in several successful business ventures in agriculture and trade, for which they used slave labour. But despite their complicity in the slave trade, the Church and the Jesuits were

21 Jeanette Pinto, *Slavery in Portuguese India*, p. 138.
22 See Anil Budur Lulla, 'A Bottle of Honey for Our Brother Prez', in Short Takes section, *Open*, 30 October 2010.

often instrumental in bettering the conditions of slaves, in sharp contrast to many other slave owners.

Slaves were generally regarded as the property of their owners with no rights of their own and the majority of slave owners subjected them to subhuman treatment. The Portuguese were known for their cruelty, punishing slaves with hot irons, whipping them with leather straps, pouring hot liquids on them, throwing pepper or salt into their eyes or punishing them by tying them to a tree and smearing their face and sensitive body parts with honey to attract red ants.[23] If slaves were tortured and killed by their owners, the cause of death was always declared as natural. If a female slave got raped, she didn't have the right to complain—only her owner could complain of 'damage to his property'. Not surprisingly, the slaves were sometimes provoked to retaliate. There are numerous reports of slaves robbing, killing and fighting citizens or each other, roaming around Goa's streets in bands.[24]

Yet despite the general decadence of Portuguese–Goan society, the colonial rulers did introduce some enlightened laws. Goan women had the right to inherit property as early as 1559, when wives, widows and girl children in the rest of India had no rights to immovable possessions, such as land and houses. This has given Goan women, even village women, a special self-confidence in claiming their share of family property. In our village, for example, one woman, her marriage having broken, moved back to her father's house after he died a few years back. Despite her brother's efforts to dislodge her with threats and verbal abuse, she took possession of one of the rooms, and there she stays, asserting her

---

23 Teotonio R. de Souza, 'Manumission of Slaves in Goa', p. 174.
24 Jeanette Pinto, *Slavery in Portuguese India*, p. 57.

right to a share in her father's property. The Portuguese also passed laws that allowed widows to remarry and stipulated that anyone obstructing a widow's remarriage would forfeit all his property, which would be divided between the widow and the king.[25] They were also progressive in the matter of women's education. These laws, however, were fuelled not by a liberal spirit, but as a means to induce women to convert to Christianity. The laws giving women the right of inheritance and encouraging widow remarriage were only effective for Christian women, or women willing to convert to Christianity. Such laws ensured that women would remain loyal subjects of the Portuguese Empire, which in turn, undertook to protect them.[26] Take the documented case of the conversion of a widow, Malamma of Gurupura (near Mangalore), who was baptized in Goa and got the viceroy as her godfather. She was rechristened Anna Maria de Saldanha. Her dead husband had bequeathed to her a considerable amount of property, movable as well as immovable, which her brothers-in-law took over. The viceroy wrote to the factor of Mangalore to see that her husband's property was restored to her.[27]

~

Looking back to the beginnings of Portuguese rule in Goa, who were the women the conquerors married? In the sixteenth century, there was a pressing need for Christian brides for

25 Arun Sinha, *Goa Indica: A Critical Portrait of Postcolonial Goa* (Delhi: Promilla Publication, 2002), p. 24.
26 Sr Emma Maria A.C., *Women in Portuguese Goa* (1510–1835) (Tellicherry: Irish, 2002), p. 107.
27 See Jeanette Pinto, *Slavery in Portuguese India*, p. 71.

Portuguese soldiers, sailors, officials—men of all classes—settled in the colonies. On a ship carrying 800 or more men, one would usually find less than ten women, sometimes none at all.[28] In the sixteenth century, Portuguese women were not even allowed to travel with their husbands, since too many would have died on the long hazardous journey, which took six to eight months.[29] There were, of course, exceptions. The first Portuguese woman was believed to have stepped on Goan soil as early as 1518—she was Dona Catarina-a-Piró, said to have been a dazzling beauty of sixteen years. She followed her lover Garcia de Sa, but died young, at the age of twenty-five. Catarina is not remembered for her virtuousness and her wedlock with Garcia was legalized only on her deathbed by none less than St Francis Xavier.[30] I drove to Old Goa on a muggy monsoon day to have a closer look at the convent of Santa Monica and to search for Dona Catarina's tomb, which is believed to be in the Church of Our Lady of the Rosary, built at the very spot where Afonso de Albuquerque conducted the naval battle against Adil Shah.[31] It was not difficult to find her tomb, a marble cenotaph with a Portuguese inscription bearing her name and begging God for compassion for her soul.

With hardly any European women around, the strategy of Afonso de Albuquerque was to foster mixed marriages of suitable Indian wives with Portuguese noblemen, sailors and soldiers, in order to establish Portuguese culture as a self-perpetuating

---

28 P.D. Gaitonde, *Portuguese Pioneers in India* (Bombay: Popular Prakashan,1983), p. 12.

29 Sr Emma Maria A.C., *Women in Portuguese Goa*, p. 99.

30 Mario Cabral E Sa, *Legends of Goa* (Bombay: India Book House Limited, 1998), p. 29.

31 Ibid., p. 29.

garrison that would protect the interests of the colonizers. The women, widows of slain Muslim soldiers and residents of the harems, had to convert to Christianity and gained upward social mobility with the marriage, while the Portuguese bridegrooms were given a number of incentives, such as land and a house, if they were willing to marry these women.[32] The mixed marriages were regarded with great ambivalence, at times even with open disapproval, by the Portuguese Crown. According to the records, there were numerous complaints about morality in Goa, arising out of the attempts to Christianize the 'Goan heathens' and to procure European women for the men in the colonies who would produce offspring for its Empire—the *Estado da Índia*. One strategy the Portuguese Crown developed and financed to strengthen their Empire, was the institution of Royal Orphans—the Orfãas d'El Rei. There was a shortage of marriageable men in Portugal, since so many had gone as soldiers and settlers to the colonies, or died young in battle or through tropical diseases, leaving behind widows and daughters who did not find 'suitable husbands' there. Many such women belonged to the nobility. These noble Portuguese orphans were sent to the colonies under the patronage of the king to be married off. The Portuguese government looked after them and also took care of their marriage expenses and their dowries. However, when the dowry was later reduced to half, due to the increasing financial problems of the Portuguese Crown, requests for marriageable women decreased and the shipping of 'suitable' orphaned girls from Portugal to the colonies gradually became less, till it ended by the mid-eighteenth century.[33]

---

32 Sr Emma Maria A.C., *Women in Portuguese Goa*, pp. 100, 106.
33 Ibid., pp. 125–6, 137, 159.

Not all the noble girls agreed to the plans of the Portuguese Crown. Once they reached the colonies, they realized that most Portuguese men in Goa were far from being *fidalgos*: they were rogues and vagrants. Some of them were even convicted criminals who had been sentenced to work on ships or had escaped from prison in Portugal. Often, girls who did not get an offer from a respectable man simply refused to get married. At that time, the only way for a girl to live a respectable life on her own was to join a convent. The problem was that not a single female convent existed in the *Estado da Índia*. Apart from the Royal Orphans, there were also wealthy, unmarried European girls or widows from all over Portuguese Asia, who had no desire to marry impoverished or debauched *fidalgos*.[34] It was these women who finally managed to persuade the Portuguese Crown to construct the first female convent in Asia: Santa Monica. This impressive building still stands in Old Goa, although it is no longer in use as a convent.

The history of Santa Monica reads like a novel, beginning with the struggles of unmarried women in setting it up and ending with the revolt of the nuns against a particular archbishop who allegedly had an insatiable sexual appetite for nuns. From 1594 till 1599 the Portuguese Crown refused all requests to build a convent, till it finally yielded in 1606. Why was there such opposition from the authorities to establishing a convent? It made me curious, but the answer is simple: among the women demanding it were a number of the Orfãas d'El Rei who had been shipped to the colony at the expense of the Crown, to marry and procreate in order to strengthen the Portuguese Empire with their offspring. Others were rich widows, such as Filipa Ferreira from Thana, who

---

34 Ibid., p. 216.

was part of the first batch of eighteen widows admitted to the convent. Filipa brought tremendous wealth and 200 slaves with her.[35] The Portuguese Crown, struggling with bankruptcy, had no reason to encourage women to live a chaste life and donate their wealth to the Church.

In the beginning, only European noblewomen were allowed entry into Santa Monica's cloistered walls. The convent grew to be a rich and important educational institution, a magnet for unmarried European women in Asia. Much later, in 1720, when there was a demand to set up a convent for local converts as well, it was refused: the Portuguese did not think it worth their while to spend their resources on single, usually indigent Goan women.[36] Today, of course, there are convents all over Goa and the nuns do admirable work to help the poor and vulnerable in the state.

The history of horses, slaves and women, all imported into Goa to serve the interests of the Portuguese ruling class at a time not too far back in the past, is a reminder of how trade and colonization have combined to make Goa such a unique melting pot of peoples, cultures and religions. Which makes me wonder why the Goa of today is comparatively more insular in its attitude to outsiders—no matter how long one has lived in Goa or how engaged one is in local life and issues, no one coming from outside will be fully accepted, unless he or she is born on Goan soil or to Goan parents.

---

35 Teotonio R. de Souza, 'Manumission of Slaves in Goa', p. 175.
36 Sr Emma Maria A.C., *Women in Portuguese Goa*, p. 214.

15

Monsoon Raga

The tourist season is coming to an end. Travellers are disappearing, beach shacks are being dismantled, and for the next four months, an empty beach and a rough sea will be all ours again. It amazes me that most outsiders who have made Goa their home leave it before the onset of the monsoon and return only after it has ended—they have no idea what they are missing.

The month before the rainy season is quite exhausting, since by April–May the humid heat becomes unbearable. The body slows down into lethargy and the brain feels like a fried egg. But April is also watermelon season, and a glass of the fresh red juice is the most delicious and cooling midday drink one can think of. Clothes, drenched with sweat, need to be changed at least twice in a day. The only relief is a cold shower or retreating into another world by lying in a hammock and reading a good book. People stock up on provisions such as dried fish to last them through the coming rainy season when fresh fish is unavailable—and for most Goans, a meal without fish is unthinkable.

Towards the end of May, one sees old Goan ladies sitting fully dressed in the shallow water near the seashore, their matronly bodies teased by the lapping waves. In Goa, it is thought that sitting in sea water in May gives relief from skin diseases, arthritis and other rheumatic illnesses, a belief that attracts people even from villages in the hinterland to the seaside. Towards June, when the heat and humidity build up with almost unbearable intensity, and everyone is longing for the monsoon to arrive, Sudhir and I usually leave the country for our annual visits to friends and family in Europe, as well as for work. We return only once the monsoon has fully set in. This is why I have seen the actual onset of the monsoon only twice—the year of our arrival, when our house was being renovated, and the second time two years later, when I was at the beach, waiting to witness what everyone assured me would be a phenomenal sight.

And what an unforgettable experience it was! I was sitting with friends at Pedro's, a beach shack on Benaulim beach which, unusually, does not shut down during the monsoon (almost all the other shacks are dismantled by April, to be rebuilt for the following tourist season in September). We must have waited for three hours, watching the dark clouds gathering at the horizon where the slate-grey sky met the ocean. The beach was full of people, talking, drinking, eating, brimming with anticipation, for this was the day the monsoon was supposed to break in Goa. We felt the breeze gradually pick up and then, suddenly, it became pitch dark. The next moment, the skies opened up and sheets of rain seemed to rush in from the sea. Moved by an atavistic impulse, we ran out of the shack and in no time everybody was drenched and dancing on the road.

The monsoon seems to possess a metallic weight and mass, as Alexander Frater describes in his book *Chasing the Monsoon*. The rain comes bucketing down, drumming on the roofs and swishing through the heavy foliage and trees.[1] It is rain of a special kind,

---

1 Alexander Frater, *Chasing the Monsoon* (New Delhi: Penguin, 1991), p. 1.

leaving behind a heavy dampness in the air, mixed with the earthy smell of Goa's red soil. The sky, bright and blue the rest of the year, becomes an alive object of observation, the imagination painting animals on the canvas of the sky.

Swollen masses of the deepest indigo blue were piled, one on top of the other, just above the horizon, looking like the puffed-out moustaches of some raging demon.[2]

Reading Tagore and Kalidasa on the veranda of our house, while the rain beats down on our tiled roof, has a special magic that amplifies the beauty of the monsoon. Sudhir sometimes plays monsoon ragas, such as Megh Malhar, when the night sets in and my untrained ear gets a vague idea of how the mood of a raga reflects the emotions evoked by this season of rain. There is eroticism, intensity, loneliness, awe.

A flight of steps, all emerald slabs—
a pool patterned over
by full-blown lotuses on glossy beryl stems
wild geese haunt its waters, freed from restless longing.[3]

There is no poetry in a Bombay monsoon with rats and garbage in flooded streets, clogged drains and dog turds disintegrating in the puddles. Here in Goa, though, the monsoon's magic is best

2 Rabindranath Tagore, *Glimpses of Bengal: Selected from the Letters of Sir Rabindranath Tagore, 1885 to 1895* (London: Macmillan, 1921), entry from 27 June 1892.
3 Kalidasa, 'Meghadutam' ('Cloud Messenger', translated by Chandra Rajan).

experienced in a safe and dry place, gazing out at a garden.

> The haze over the sky makes the moon look like a sleepy eye kept open.[4]

A calmness settles in while I look out into the night, listening to the sounds of the rain. Sudhir is smoking his cigar, little is said; we feel an ineffable peace flow through our bodies and minds.

> Many such evenings may come, but they may refuse to nestle so trustfully, so lovingly, with such complete abandon, to my breast.[5]

We continue sitting on the veranda with glasses of wine, while the heavy rain falls like a curtain of glass from the edge of the roof; a spray blown in by the winds, moistening our faces and the naked skin of our arms.

The rains restore various shades of green to the landscape, from a shy bamboo-green to a deep bottle-green; plants seem to grow overnight. All the senses are sharpened, the transformation of the dry earth into a green jungle heightening one's alertness to sounds, smells and sights. During the monsoon, I usually encounter many more snakes in our garden, all of them (so far) harmless beautiful creatures. I wonder in how many compounds of traditional Hindu houses a lamp is still lit in honour of the 'snake of the place', the guardian of the garden, a practice very common in the olden days in Goa and still very popular in Kerala, where it is called 'sarpkavus'.

---

4 Rabindranath Tagore, *Glimpses of Bengal*, entry from 9 January 1892.
5 Ibid., entry from 16 May 1893.

Over all, the storm droned like a giant snake-charmer's pipe, and to its rhythm swayed hundreds and thousands of crested waves, like so many hooded snakes. The thunder was incessant, as though a whole world was being pounded to pieces away there behind the clouds.[6]

After nightfall, every corner in the garden seems to come alive. Crickets chirp so loudly that at times their high-pitched chorus hurts the ears. They seem to be in competition with an army of frogs in the mood for mating. When the frogs lay their eggs in the swimming pool, I rescue the white froth in the morning and put it into a bucket of water. I then wait till the tiny tadpoles hatch, usually after five or six days. Once they have hatched, I put them into the water of our fountain and, if there are too many, into a nearby pond. My husband is amused by my mothering care for generations of tadpoles, while Kailash expresses his disgust without saying a word.

All last night the wind howled like a stray dog, and the rain still pours on without a break.[7]

Monsoon is a time for flooded fields and days spent inside the house; a time for inner stillness, when unwinding is easy. It is also a time for fresh roasted cashew nuts, for beach walks in the rain . . . and for viral infections. It is a time for feasts and vibrant festivals that follow one another. One of these, Sao Joao, the fertility feast of St John the Baptist, usually takes place at the end of June when the

---

6 Ibid., entry from June 1891.
7 Ibid., entry from 3 July 1893.

rains are in full swing. I am not sure how many villagers remember that Sao Joao actually celebrates the biblical story where Mary visits Elizabeth, the mother of St John. On this day, the young men of the village jump into overflowing wells to retrieve feni bottles hidden in their depths by their owners. I have rarely seen village youngsters having more fun than during this part of the festival. The San Joao festival, thankfully, has not become commercialized like the Carnival with its tacky floats and teeming crowds. In many villages tucked away in Goa's hinterlands such unique festivals are still celebrated in more or less the same way as they have been for generations. Music, feni and fun are as much part of these festivals as praying, and it's also an occasion to create *kopels*—crowns most beautifully fashioned out of flowers, berries and leaves. Another festival unique to Goa in this season is the monsoon cucumber feast, Touxeanchem. This is celebrated in the Church of Santa Ana in Talaulim, where people, especially couples hoping for a child, buy freshly harvested cucumbers from vendors in front of the church and then give them as offerings. I do not need to quote my husband here on the symbolism of the cucumber.

> A cloud embracing the crest of the hill
> strikingly-shaped like a sportive elephant
> bent down to butt a river bank.[8]

I had never imagined that I could develop such a passion for the rains, that the monsoon would become my favourite season. It is a time when Goa is empty of the Western tourists that throng this small state the rest of the year. Goa's monsoon tourism, however,

---

8 Kalidasa, 'Meghadutam'.

is now on the rise, with the rains attracting not just tourists from other parts of India, taking advantage of inexpensive packages for long weekends offered by hotels, but also the 'desert people' from the Gulf countries immersing themselves in what is for them a rare and rejuvenating experience.

Goa looks spotlessly clean during the monsoons, because the ubiquitous garbage heaps that disfigure the landscape are overgrown by creepers and bushes. The sea looks pristine and powerful in its emptiness, as there are no fishing boats and trawlers to be seen—fishing is prohibited during these three months in order to allow the fish to breed. It is a time when the soil is scented and new life emerges from everywhere.

The sheer amount of rain—the average annual rainfall in Goa is more than three metres—coursing down the roads and lanes, filling the fields, lakes, wells and canals, seems to wash away all the decay and detritus that accumulate through the year. And the waterfalls located in Goa's serene countryside, at Dudhsagar, Netravali, Hivrem and Kesarval, though not so easy to reach, are a truly magnificent sight.

It can be entertaining to watch how the locals go about their daily lives during the monsoons—pedalling their bicycles, one arm on the handlebar and the other holding up a black umbrella, or ingeniously using plastic sheets and plastic bags to keep themselves dry. Yet these efforts help little, because when it rains here, it pours. I find it impossible to predict a rain shower. There are moments when I look up at the sky, thinking it will rain any minute and, half an hour later, it is still dry. At other times, my dog Maya and I just start to walk on the beach, certain that the clouds are far off, only to find ourselves racing back to the car five minutes later. But getting drenched here in a sudden shower feels almost therapeutic, as long as the rain is warm and soothing.

When I experienced my first monsoon in Goa, I wondered what people wore to protect themselves against the rain before plastic was invented. The mystery was solved one day, when in the interior of Goa, I saw two women walking on the road under a kind of body shield made of coconut leaves and worn on the head. It looked like a funny kind of turtle shell that covered the head, back and sides of the body. The women must have come from the fields, because later I learned that this protective covering that looked as strong as a coat of armour is called a *konddo* and is frequently used while planting paddy when the hands need to be free. I was impressed by such a simple and 'organic' solution!

> There was a break in the rains yesterday, but the clouds are banked up so heavily along the skirts of the sky [. . .] It looks as if a heavy carpet of cloud has been rolled up to one side, and at any moment a fussy breeze may come along and spread it over the whole place again.[9]

By September, the rains taper off and the showers become infrequent. Slowly, the urge to see the sun becomes stronger. The dampness of all these months can be smelt in the mildew on clothes, bedsheets and towels. Fungus covers shoes and books.

I wonder where the butterflies, such fragile beings, which now reappear in profusion in our garden, hide when there is an occasional shower. They miraculously flutter around as soon as there is a break in the rain and disappear before the next shower

---

9 Rabindranath Tagore, *Glimpses of Bengal*, entry from 4 July 1893.

arrives. In one of the tribal areas nearby, there is a sacred grove known for its beautiful butterflies that appear right after the monsoon ends, ethereally lovely symbols of the change of seasons.

After four months of rain, the sun and heat are welcome. It has been our tenth monsoon in Goa, and for me, it has lost none of its magic: a season that is at once terrifying, wonderful, a blessing, a mystery.

16

How Foreign Is Foreign?

When we moved to Goa, I was not aware that many Goans harbour a deep-rooted suspicion towards 'outsiders', whether foreigners or Indians from other states. As in most cultures, here too there are different expressions for the 'other', the foreigner. In Konkani, Goa's state language, the most widely used terms are bhaile (outsider) and ghanti (people from over the ghats).

In Goa's chequered history, the land has been occupied innumerable times by foreign rulers, such as the Mauryas, the Bhojas, the Chalukyas, the Kadambas, the Devagiri Yadavas, the Vijayanagara Empire, the Bahmani Sultanate and the Bijapur Sultanate to name some. Goa has for centuries been a melting pot where many cultures left their imprint. As the scholar Antonio Mascarenhas has rightly observed, 'Goan culture is the product of distillation of many cultural identities'.[1] From that perspective, all Goans, with the exception of the tribal population, are 'outsiders', even the Saraswat Brahmins who settled in Goa at some remote period of their history.

While the general term for outsider, bhaile, refers to people like my husband and I (fairly well-to-do, educated Indians and foreigners), the term ghanti defines migrant workers from other

---

1 See Mario Cabral E Sa, 'Of Goan, Pro-Goan and Maha-Bhaile', in *Gomantak Times*, 22 April 2008, p. A8.

Indian states. Though neither expression, when used by Goans, can be considered flattering, the latter is much more pejorative: the phrase so and so 'behaves like a ghanti', is equated with someone being an uncouth idiot. A ghanti will have a hard time being accepted and integrated into the Goan fold, even though Goans depend heavily on migrant workers from states like Bihar, Orissa and Jharkhand to do all the hard work that most Goans (and bhailes like us, who have settled here) are not prepared to do themselves. Whether it is construction work, gardening, serving in restaurants or working on the fishing trawlers, most hard labour and low-income jobs are done by non-Goans. Many of the educated Goan youth go abroad for professional opportunities, while young Goans with a limited education stay behind, often jobless. Even if offered work, for example, as carpenters, bakers or waiters, they are not prepared to take it up. 'Either they don't want the jobs for which they have the skills, or they don't have the skills for the jobs they want.'[2] Instead they dream of leaving the country for better-paid jobs in the Gulf, or on cruise ships. A few manage to do so; the others hang around the village centres doing nothing. They can afford not to work, because in every Goan family one or more 'slog outside the country and send money home, while others at home sit and enjoy that money in luxury unemployment'.[3]

Thus, the older generation of Goan carpenters, masons, plumbers and others in similar trades now relies on support staff from outside Goa to keep businesses running. Despite the dearth

2 Arun Sinha, *Goa Indica: A Critical Portrait of Postcolonial Goa* (Delhi: Promilla Publication, 2002).
3 The term 'luxury unemployment' was coined by Errol D'Souza. See Arun Sinha, p. 179.

of local skilled labour and the pressing need for migrant workers, many Goans resent—and some even harbour hostile feelings towards—the growing population of poorer migrants. These ghantis are accused of being responsible for the rising crime rate (though the vast majority sitting in Aguada jail are Goans). Many migrants live in illegal slum settlements and attract the ire of Goans who feel that they are favoured by politicians as vote banks and thus get ration cards and other government subsidies more easily than common Goans. There is even a growing demand for controlling or banning migrant workers from settling here, fuelled by the fear that Goans will soon become a minority in their own state. This fear is echoed in media comments, such as in Mario Cabral E Sa's remark in one of his newspaper columns that the Goan, like the dodo is a (nearly) extinct species. The well-known Konkani writer Damodar Mauzo explains, 'Migrants settling in our neighbouring states Maharashtra and Karnataka don't make a difference to the population, since millions of people live there, but Goa is such a small place that demographics change significantly with the influx of migrant workers. This is why people feel insecure.' In the 1960s, Goa's population was around 600,000. Today (though estimates vary), the population has more than doubled, of which around 40 per cent are outsiders, mainly migrant workers.

Goans are resentful that the outsiders who come and swamp their countryside often have little respect for the culture and values of their chosen home. The industrialist Raj Salgaocar points out that the debate on 'Goanity' should not be about Goan versus non-Goan, but about people's state of mind: how receptive or ignorant they are of Goan customs and traditions, and what their contribution is to society. The writer Savia Viegas takes a similar view: 'The time has come to redefine terms like bhitorle (insiders) and bhaile (outsiders) since one cannot help but notice that bhitorle are acting more like bhaile, least concerned about Goa's future.'[4] Like them, there are other Goans who take a clear position when the question 'Who is a Goan?' is raised. 'It's the love for Goa that makes you a Goan, you need to have a passion for the place,' says Yogini Acharya, a Goan psychologist writing on Goan identity. 'Anyone who contributes to the wellbeing of Goa is a Goan, hence the question of bhaile does not exist,' reads a comment on the Goan Forum in an online interview.[5] According to Anwesha Singbal, a young Goan Hindu, assimilation is a vital factor: those who 'are in sync with the local culture will be accepted'. Or, as Raj Salgaocar puts it, 'Once a "bhaile" imbibes Goanness in his persona, he becomes a "Goenkar".'

However, for most Goans, their identity is rooted in blood, or 'ethnic Goan descent', playing out what Vidyadhar Gadgil calls the 'insider' versus 'outsider' game.[6] A Goan who has lived abroad all his life without much connection with his motherland is more likely to be embraced as an 'insider' than any bhaile living in Goa and loving it, no matter how deeply he or she is connected to the place and its people.

I think it is about time this sterile insider–outsider debate on

4 Walter Menezes, 'Who Is an "Insider", Who Is an "Outsider" . . . Language Etc', in Goanet News, 27 July 2011 (http://lists.goanet.org/pipermail/goanet-news-goanet.org/2011-July/004319.html).

5 The Goan Forum, 'Goa Going Gone', January 2004 (http://www.colaco.net/1/TGFresponds2igoNoJobsForGoans.htm).

6 Vidyadhar Gadgil, 'Garv se Kaho Hum Ghanti Hain!'. *Inside/Out— New Writing From Goa*. Edited by Helene Derkin Menezes and Jose Lourenco (Saligao: Goa 1556 and Goa writers, 2011), p. 54.

'who is Goan and who is not' is brought to an end. In the years I have lived here, I have got the impression that the debate on 'Goanity' has become more emotional and less fact based. There is a real anxiety that the growing number of outsiders will have too much of an undesirable impact on Goan values and culture. The Catholic community seems particularly insecure about the influx of outsiders because, as the writer Maria Couto framed it, 'their way of life is probably more threatened'. The Catholic elite still mourns the loss of their privileges with the departure of the Portuguese sixty years ago. Further, with the influx of migrants, who are mainly Hindu and Muslim, and with many Goan Catholics moving abroad, the concentration of Catholics in the state has shrunk significantly from 40 per cent in the 1960s to around 24 per cent today. Among the Catholics there is also an increasing nostalgia for a lost era, which is reflected in Lord Meghnad Desai's remark about Goa's famous cartoonist, the late Mario Miranda: 'Here was a man who was Goan, Indian, and a citizen of the world. He could not be what he was had he not been Goan . . . The crucial thing is that Liberation should not erase the Portuguese influence so thoroughly that a second Mario Miranda will never thrill us. That would be a tragedy.'[7]

Meghnad Desai's remark pinpoints how Goans feel about themselves: that the unique confluence of cultures and traditions in their home state has contributed to their unique identity and personality, setting them apart from other Indians. As Raj Salgaocar observes, 'Goan identity is a multilayered identity which we have developed over thousands of years, giving Goans a distinct way of life. Our identity is based on our geography and

---

7 See 'Liberation Blues', in *Times of India*, 1 January 2012, p. 5.

history, on a myriad of influences over the years.' Maria Couto adds that political policies of the nineteenth century, which gave rights of citizenship and equal rights to women, added to the strong sense of identity possessed by Goans.

Post-Liberation, a development that has had an unsettling impact on the Goan mind is the fact that Goa's government, when it comes to the top ranks of the administration, is mainly run by Indians from other states, who are better qualified for these positions. So, in a strange way, one could provocatively aver that Goa is still ruled by 'foreigners'—civil servants from other states, who often do not even speak Konkani. As Damodar Mauzo remarks, many Goans felt after Liberation that the governance of their state was in the hands of the wrong people. He recounts that the level of corruption seen in Goa today never existed before outsiders, mainly Maharashtrians, took over the top administrative positions. There is unease that the Goan is represented inadequately within his own state and thus has no control over his state's development. Perhaps, having dealt with foreign rulers throughout history, there is 'a certain degree of resistance to any outsider dictating what is right for you', says Yogini Acharya. 'Even if their contributions are positive, most Goans wouldn't take it from an outsider.' Outsiders often label Goans as laid-back, not too interested in working hard or making an effort—a perception that does not sit well with Goans. Says Anwesha Singbal, 'I would consider Goans to be a bit relaxed, but I would not mock them by saying "susegad" because that often indicates that Goans do not believe in hard work. The fact is Goans are a self-satisfied chunk of people who are ambitious, but not over-ambitious.' Maria Couto feels, 'It looks as if Goans are not concerned about the quality of life. Quality of life for a

Goan requires a certain element of leisure. There is a pattern, a rhythm to daily life in Goa, which is combined with leisure. To equate susegad with laid-back is a mistranslation by the English-speaking world. Goans would never call it laid-back.' She adds, 'Susegad, coming from the Portuguese word "sossego", means peace, quiet and, by implication, "peace of mind". And there is nothing as conducive and peaceful as the Goan landscape.'

Most Goans find it difficult to accept the developments of the past twenty years and the impact that globalization and tourism have had on their small state. Nevertheless, the state depends on tourism, earning Rs 10,000 crore in foreign exchange annually. There is a growing nostalgia for the 'good old days' under Portuguese rule when law and order worked and people were more civilized and less greedy. I have more than once heard remarks to the effect that it would have been better if the Portuguese had stayed on. This nostalgia relates to what Damodar Mauzo describes as 'the low crime rate, the susegad lifestyle, the afternoon siesta, the sense of security that existed then . . . all these factors are often cited as the virtues of our Portuguese past. "*Te Firangi Gele, Te Undde Gele* (Gone are the Portuguese, Gone are the *pão*-bread)" is a proverb often used in the same sense.' Some Goans feel the Liberation from Portuguese rule liberated them of their jobs, land and way of life.

However, few Goans are willing to reflect upon their own contribution to the present situation and would rather blame the bhailes for anything that goes wrong in the state, especially when it comes to the sale of land and the rapid cultural and social changes that Goan society is confronted with. Though it is Goans who sell their land to outsiders, or act as brokers, there is a big outcry about the bhaile onslaught on Goan property. The property issue points to the importance of land with regard to Goan identity.

Having lived here for ten years now, I realize that 'Goanity' is framed by two defining themes: land and language.

'Generations had cultivated the lands, nurtured the coconut groves, built the irrigation systems and enjoyed the produce of the land, the catch of the sea, the monsoon and the breeze,' writes Arun Sinha.[8] The importance of 'land' in the Goan mind derives not only from its fertility and beauty, but also from the fact that Goa has always been an agricultural community, where—as Maria Couto points out—'everybody, whether rich or poor, worked the land'. People had—and still have—a deep connection to their villages and the village communities used to be tightly knit together through a system called 'comunidades'. Compared to the rest of southern India, where land rights were largely connected to royal privilege, there are only a few land rights in Goa that can be traced back to kings, comment the scholars Axelrod and Fuerch. 'In Goa, both before and after the arrival of the Portuguese, land was largely in the hands of the two dominant castes, the Gaud Saraswat Brahmans ... and Marathas.'[9] They are the hereditary shareholders of this unique system of collective landownership, and divide profits and losses of income from the land. Governed by these castes, comunidades land as an ancient socio-agro-economic institution was the equivalent of a self-governing village cooperative with absolute landownership rights. Most of the paddy crop, Goa's staple food, was grown that way and the temple (in earlier times) was the central meeting point. As the late Konkani writer Chandrakant

---

8 See 'Liberation Blues', in *Times of India*, 1 January 2012, p. 5.
9 P. Axelrod/M.A. Fuerch, 'Flight of the Deities: Hindu Resistance in Portuguese Goa'. *Modern Asian Studies* (Cambridge: Cambridge University Press, May 1996) Vol. 30(2), p. 402.

Keni has observed, 'The people functioned under the harmony produced by the village *Gram Samstha*, or council of 10 elders, and the village temple. While the Gram Samstha generally met in the temple precincts and settled all disputes, the village deity was the strong bond that helped unite the community irrespective of their caste.'[10]

Closely linked to family temples or, for converted Christians, village churches, land and harvest created a strong attachment to one's village and community. Till today, Goans from all over the world come together once a year to celebrate the feast of their deity. One can observe a religious crossover at church and temple feasts in Goa, which is a unique phenomenon linked to the destruction of Hindu temples before and during the Inquisition. As I have mentioned earlier, there are Christians who visit their former family temples once a year, and Hindus who visit certain churches at places where important temples once stood. Take, for example, the Colva church with its famed Baby Jesus statue. A Bal Krishna temple once existed where the church now stands. Many Hindus come to the annual church feast described in Chapter 7, even though they may have forgotten the link to the Bal Krishna temple. Tradition makes them continue to come to the Colva feast each year. Another example is the Holy Cross in Bambolim, which stands next to the highway, a so-called 'miracle place' that gained importance in the 1950s when people leaving Goa made a vow at the cross and came back later to make offerings after their vow was fulfilled. Today Christians, Muslims and Hindus

---

10 I owe this quote to Raj Salgaocar from 'Goan Identity and Diaspora' by Chandrakant Keni, *Goa Aparanta—Land Beyond the End*. Edited by Victor Rangel-Ribeiro (Panaji: Goa Publications, 2008), p. 200.

pray here. I was told that many young Hindu students pray at the crucifix before exams for good results. Every time I pass the church on my way to north Goa, the place is crowded with flowers and people praying. Another miracle cross, which is venerated by Goan Christians, Hindus and Muslims alike, is the one in Betul. On drives through the countryside, I always take my visitors there, since the cross is located on a hill which has a splendid view of the countryside. There are many other places of shared faith, such as the Damodar temple in Zambaulim, which even has a special space for Christians to receive *prasad*. Indeed, in this temple, Christians are always the first to receive prasad from the Hindu priests. In Mapusa, the Christian mother goddess Larai has a Hindu sister goddess, and both communities exchange gifts on feast days. Some folk songs also reflect the nature of this shared faith. Damodar Mauzo gave me an example of a popular song, sung by both communities—the songs are identical except that the name of the Hindu goddess changes to Saina Bahin, the Christian Mother Mary.

There is another feature unique to Goa. Due to its small size, there has never been a true divide between 'urban' and 'rural' that one finds elsewhere in India. There is a significant percentage of middle-class families living in Goan villages and even those who live in towns often go back to their villages, which are closely connected to neighbouring towns. 'Goan villages tell an altogether different story of rural life: high culture, a greater degree of Europeanization, and a more austere form of Christianity,' writes Maria Couto.[11] Deep down, the Goan is rooted to his village,

---

11 Maria Aurora Couto, *Goa: A Daughter's Story*, (New Delhi: Penguin, 2004), p. xiii.

which is both deeply conservative and, unlike villages elsewhere in India, very modern.

Though they have travelled extensively, and the number of Goans who have migrated exceeds the number of Goans living in the state, most Goans today would not like to move, often not even out of their village. 'I would never leave Goa, not even for the best of offers. I feel I can do so much in this tiny land of mine, for my language and for my culture. My creativity would end if I step out of here,' says Anwesha Singbal, reflecting the feelings of many young educated Goans today.

Language is as strong a factor as land and village in defining identity for a Goan. Konkani, Goa's mother tongue, is a glue that has kept all Goans united, though it was banned by a decree in 1684. Portuguese was the medium of instruction at that time, but Konkani continued to remain the lingua franca of the common man despite the ban. However, the upper class spoke Portuguese with their children and Konkani with servants. So Konkani became the language of the servants and thus lost its status. This has long since changed. Goans today take pride in speaking Konkani, though it remains a spoken language with many different dialects, depending on which part of Goa one lives in. While Marathi remained the language of education, Konkani is the language of identity and the language of the church, since most church services across Goa are held in Konkani. It is a kind of a paradox: Goans speak Konkani, but read Marathi. There are different Marathi newspapers available in Goa but, to my knowledge, only one in Konkani. There are excellent contemporary Konkani writers, such as Damodar Mauzo, but the language of literature remains Marathi. Many Goan Hindus are well read in Marathi and can express themselves better in that language, although the younger generation, as my Goan friends confirm, can no longer speak or read it properly. This is a great loss, since Marathi literature has a long history and much to offer.

After Independence, Konkani became an important tool to assert the identity of the Goans. The Indian government had a political interest, after the Liberation, in merging Goa with Maharashtra. Thus, Marathi was pushed as a language and almost all teachers at that time came from Maharashtra. And so, after the Liberation, all Hindus were taught by Marathi teachers. However, none of the Catholics joined the schools. When the referendum was held on whether Goa should merge with Maharashtra or remain an independent state, the Hindu and Christian communities united and the majority of Goans voted for a separate state with Konkani as their state language. Their battle cry was '*Amchem Goem Amka Zai* (We Want Goa for Goans)'. The vote against a merger with Maharashtra was a huge achievement for the Goan people, especially Catholics, whose interests and identity would have been submerged in a big state like Maharashtra. This victory should not be underestimated and explains why language and land—Goa being such a small, distinct state—are of such significance for its residents' identity. Damodar Mauzo comments, 'We are proud of our Goan culture. We had to struggle hard to protect it. So far, we have preserved our distinct identity, both political and cultural, and shall strive to retain that title "different" for posterity.'[12]

For me, Goan culture is the culture of an anchored and

12 Damodar Mauzo, 'Goa is Different', in *The Goan*, 20 October 2012, (http://www.thegoan.net//Semana-da-Cultura-IndoPortuguesa/Goa-is-different/01532.html).

contented people, with a love of dance, music and theatre. Humour runs in their blood, and good food and convivial company always seem available in abundance. With Goa's gentle and beautiful countryside, its alluring ocean and its warm tropical climate, it is not surprising that so many well-to-do Indians buy property and move to Goa. I am not talking about the many Delhiites and Mumbaikars who buy holiday homes in Goa, visiting just once or twice and leaving them locked up the rest of the year. For many of them it seems more important to mention at parties that they own a place in Goa, than to actually be there.

I am speaking of Indians and foreigners who come here for reasons other than holidaying, many of them leading creative lives as artists, writers or designers. The author Kishwar Desai, who owns a 400-year-old house in Loutolim, comes here periodically to write, because 'it's one of the most cosmopolitan states in the country, and people are used to a mix of cultures and languages, so it's very easy to integrate'. Both she and her husband, Meghnad Desai, find the atmosphere very conducive to their creative pursuits. For her, as for many others, it is the relaxed way of life, the greenery, the absence of stress and the hectic pace of big-city life, and the sheer beauty of the land, not to speak of the safety of leaving doors unlocked, that draw them to Goa to work.

Many well-known Indian artists have made Goa their second home. The internationally acclaimed photographer Dayanita Singh was one of the first to buy a house and work here periodically. Someone once made a pithy observation about her house in Saligao, which looks like a piece of art the way Dayanita has furnished it and utilized its wall and garden space: 'It feels like walking into one of her pictures.' An online feature observes that Goa has made a huge difference to Dayanita's creativity and has led to a new series of minimalistic works which are devoid of human presence. 'Living in a Goan village has shaped her art in unexpected ways,' writes Frederick Noronha, 'so much so that she has now surprised those familiar with her work by coming out with photographs that simply don't have people in them.'

When asked why she chose Goa, artist, production designer and documentary film-maker Aradhana Seth, who used to come here regularly to work before setting up her own place, replied, 'Calm, time, waves.' The growing community of creative people settling in Goa has drawn others too: famed sculptor Radhakrishnan bought a house in Goa with the intention of working here on his striking bronze sculptures. However, Goa didn't quite work out for him—he found neither skilled support staff nor the right kind of understanding or appreciation for his work. He has now relocated to Santiniketan and only comes to Goa to relax and enjoy its peace.

A few years back, Amitav Ghosh and his wife, Deborah Baker, both writers, renovated a house in Aldona and now divide their time between New York, Calcutta and Goa. The academic Sunil Khilnani and his wife, Katherine Boo, whose book *Behind the Beautiful Forevers* has won international acclaim, have a house here too. The Booker Prize-winning novelist Kiran Desai returns to Goa regularly to have uninterrupted time to work on her novels. When I met her recently, she was in the company of her mother, Anita Desai, an acclaimed author herself. There are many other creative souls who would like to come and stay here part of the year, such as the pop artiste Ketna Patel and her husband, Jon, who had contemplated settling part-time in Goa, but could not find an affordable house. All these people, however, come only for part of the year and Goa for them is a second home.

Far less usual is to find outsiders like Sudhir and me, who have no other base but Goa, spending most of the year here except when we travel within and out of India. Other Indians too have made the big jump in a courageous attempt to redefine their lives. They've given up old professions, moved to Goa and started something different, closer to their heart. One such person is the lawyer Diviya Kapur, who moved to Goa to open a bookshop-cafe in an old house in Calangute, which now is a charming and popular meeting place in north Goa. 'Here you can taste and smell and feel as if abroad, but you are not. You are still in India,' says Diviya in an interview with Aimee Ginsburg,[13] implying that the Goan way of life is difficult to find or replicate in other parts of India. Goa's soothing landscape and climate, its combination of country life and city pleasures within easy reach, its friendly people, its abundance of good restaurants and bars, its relatively liberal social attitudes, its good Internet connectivity even in villages and the abundance of flight connections that make it easy to get in and out of Goa—all these combine to make many Indians feel that in Goa they have most of the allures of life abroad, with the comforts and familiarity of life in India.

This feeling of living at an intersection of Western and Indian cultures also attracts Europeans who come to pursue professional opportunities and embrace the creative space Goa offers. My German friend Alice, a designer, who creates her own collection of clothes and, as an interior architect, furnishes the homes of the wealthy, moved to Sangolda because she could afford to buy and renovate a beautiful old house there, something that would have

---

13 Aimee Ginsburg, 'The Great Escape', in *India Today*, 5 December 2007 (http://indiatoday.intoday.in/story/The+great+escape/1/2226.html).

been impossible in her home country. She chose Goa also because it offered her professional opportunities in an environment that allows for diversity. Alice feels she can live her creativity in a way that would not be possible in Europe.

Another dear friend, Charlotte Hayward, is from England, but was born in India and spent a part of her childhood in Calcutta. She, along with her brother Simon, opened a charming and successful boutique hotel called Vivenda Dos Palhacos in Majorda. Whenever I drop in for a glass of wine or am invited for a meal, I meet guests who are special and interesting to talk to. For Charlotte, 'India feels more potent than "the West".' She continues, 'Living and working in Goa is frustrating and yet fulfilling as there is freedom from public opinion, regulations and critics, which is liberating and supportive, enabling the beginning of creative projects, as this process is less daunting than in the West. There are, of course, endless hurdles and hysterical setbacks that are unforeseeable, and therefore unexpected, but eventually, the real possibility of accomplishing projects tips the balance in favour of Goa.'

One can live in a village in Goa, have a cool, modern and open way of life, with the many advantages of a metropolis and none of its disadvantages. For many outsiders settling part-time, it is also important that Goa already has a 'critical mass' of Indians and foreigners living here, making it easy for 'newcomers' to connect and feel at home. Its small size adds to the attraction: one can meet up easily with friends, no matter which part of Goa one lives in.

Although most Goans I have met and befriended are the most hospitable, welcoming and accepting folks, quite a few outsiders have told me that they often feel hurt, disappointed or frustrated with the attitudes of Goans towards their success, or by the lack of appreciation for the hard work they have put in to succeed. One of my foreign friends, who ran a flourishing restaurant in Goa, but moved back to Europe after a few years, once said, 'My success does not come from a vacuum. I work very, very hard for it. People don't want to see that. I am sick and tired of dealing with their envy.' My friend's complaint is not without cause. Successful foreigners in Goa often invite disdain and envy from locals. Goans are a very talented people, successful in their chosen professions all over the world, so why not be more generous towards outsiders making the most of *their* talents here?

Having lived for almost a decade in Goa now, I am an outsider everywhere, even in the country I was born and brought up in. But this outsider tag can be quite liberating. I perceive many things from a certain distance. I do not need to identify too strongly with 'insider' issues, whether it is in my home country or here, and I feel easily at home wherever I go. Since bhailes like me are to a certain degree already ostracized, no one bothers too much whether or not you follow social norms, as long as you do not stick your neck out too much. My husband, Sudhir, once said, 'There are people who grow roots, unhappy if they have to move. And there are people like you—they are birds that fly from tree to tree. They build their homes in them, but move on, if necessary. For them, the sky is also home.'

Acknowledgements

Exploring my chosen home has taken me to places and to meetings with people who have enriched my life. I am deeply grateful for the hospitality and openness of so many Goans who were so generous with their time and help while writing this book. It is impossible to name all of them personally. However, special thanks go to my friend Anne Bäumele-Afonso, who accompanied me on a number of trips to places that are relevant in this book.

I am greatly indebted to Nandini Mehta, my editor at Penguin, for her encouragement and close reading of the manuscript. Her inputs in giving final shape to this book were invaluable. I would further like to thank my friend Subodh Kerkar for reading the manuscript and giving me valuable leads and insights. Last but not least, I am grateful to my husband, Sudhir Kakar, who is always my first reader. The many conversations we shared, his perspective, love and generosity have given me confidence and all the support needed to sit and write this book . . .

To all who have contributed and helped, 'tujen Dev beren koro!'—'may God treat you well, thank you!'